Devon Church Walks

(North and East)

28 Walks

Published by *PP (Pé Publishing)*
Email: tonyhlape12@gmail.com

ISBN: 978-0-9543690-8-8

Maps: John Avenell. Reproduced by permission of Ordnance Survey or behalf of the Controller of Her Majesty`s Stationery Office, © Crow Copyright
Cover Illustration: Audrey Stevens
Photographs: Diana Pé, David Perks and Bonita Tully
Artwork Production: Den Clarke
Printed by: Downland Print Services Ltd, 2015

Acknowledgements: My thanks for their help in the preparation of th book go to John Avenell, Christiane Good, Windy Leung, Anne Parke Gabrielle and Robert Pé and Giselle, Tony Pé, David Perks, Pam Smitl Audrey Stevens, Peggy Synge, Nicky Thornhill, and Bonita Tully.

I dedicate this book to my friend, Doreen Peskett who shared h knowledge of Nature with me and her love of village churches.

Preface

Regular visitors to Devon come to the county with a mixture of affection and awe. Devonshire has so much natural beauty, so many daunting hills and secluded vales, rich plateaux, wide seascapes and little bays. There are two contrasting coasts: wild and remote in the north; long and varied in the south.

Variety is one of Devon`s main attributes. The very soil is varied; old stones have produced rich culm, then there are four other sandstones, chalk, limestone, red clay and granite. Exeter is at the centre of the contrasting scenery that these stones create. It is also the religious and political capital.

Plymouth is the coastal capital of a seafaring people. Apart from these two, there are few big towns. Axminster in the east and Tavistock in the west are so far apart they emphasize the large extent of the county. In the centre, Crediton has been overtaken by Exeter, and Cullompton by Tiverton. Barnstaple has maintained its dominance in the north – just, for Bideford is a close rival. In the south Totnes has become a cultural centre. We cannot ignore the sprawling Torbay conurbation for retirement and holidays on the south coast and some good walks start there.

Towns and villages are generally far apart. The intervening space is mainly devoted to agriculture. Travellers remember the long, narrow winding lanes, buried deep in hedgerows, bringing them to an exquisite village or lone farm – it may not be the place they were looking for but it is so lovely, the hazards of the travel are worthwhile. Once you have found the starting point for some of the walks in these two books, I hope they help you to unravel some of the ways to church.

Central to each town and village is the parish church often built of local stone. A distinguishing feature of Devon churches can be seen in wooden carvings on myriad styles of screen and unique bench ends. You will also find long wagon roofs, ancient fonts, beautiful windows and welcoming porches. So many medieval churches, cherished by succeeding generations of Devon men and women, open their doors to the respectful visitor.

I am only sorry I have not included more. There is material here for two more books at least but someone else will have to find the paths, tracks and lanes that I have not taken to the churches I have yet to visit.

Maps: Once again John Avenell has valiently carried on producing carefully clear maps, a double whammy this time, for there are two Devon books!
Covers: Audrey Stevens has chosen a scene from Ilfracombe for the North Devon book and an iconic view of Dartmouth for South Devon. Thank you!

Devon Church Walks

North and East

Location Map

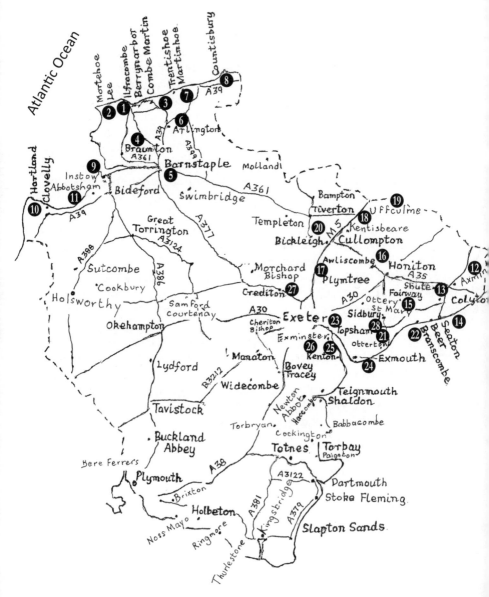

Contents

Introduction

See the end of 'South and West Devon Walks' for long distance paths

Introduction 'Dire Devon' – St Aldhelm

Devon was always going to be a challenge. I have left it `til last, fearful of its size, hills, its climate and its notorious lanes. I have not been disappointed. Rivers abound: the Axe, the Exe, the Otter, the Dart, the Plym, the Tavy and the Tamar in the south alone. They enter the English Channel at famous ports and holiday resorts where the South West Coast Path acknowledges ramblers. Footpaths are harder to find if you follow the rivers inland to join their numerous tributaries through beautiful but boggy scenery. The problem is compounded by the relentless domination of agriculture. The farmer rules. He will drive his herd along a dirt track that happens to be a footpath and the rambler has to cope with the ensuing quagmire. 'High hedge banks prevent the lanes from drying out, for several months of the year there is deep and liquid mud' - W.J. Hoskins *Devon.*

Before you despair, I hasten to claim that I have planned and puzzled to find ways through to some of the most extraordinary and unexpected churches in villages where time has stood still. I have even unearthed treasures hitherto unpublished. Sometimes, this has necessitated walking along the road for a while. Luckily only the occasional car driver ventures on these roads where his or her speed is restricted by the steep slopes and succession of sharp bends.

And, I can truly confirm that the **Devonshire folk are the salt of the earth**. Visitors from the four corners of the world will be welcomed. There is nothing narrow or standoffish about the inhabitants of Devon. Of course they have had their own spate of exploring. No county can have produced so many famous sailors, adventurers, explorers and pirates. Remember John Hawley (1379), John Hawkins (1532), Francis Drake (1540), Richard Grenville (1542), Walter Raleigh (1540), William Bligh (1754) to name a few. James Templer (B1722), an orphan who ran away to sea and made a fortune in India. He returned to buy and renovate the Stover Estate, Newton Abbot. His son built the Stover Canal to carry clay to River Teign for export. His grandson George built the granite tramway from Haytor to link with the canal. It carried granite from Dartmoor quarries to the canal and beyond. More recently, John H, Speke and Richard F. Burton set off in search of the source of the Nile and discovered Tanganyika in 1858.

But we have to discover Devonshire and its thousands of churches – or some of them. Regretfully, I always have to omit too many. They will still be there for other explorers.

The Early Church

As in Cornwall, wayside crosses and shrines were the first gathering points established by pilgrims who brought Christianity to Devon. Tawstock has a holy well in the village, suggesting Celtic forbears, lost in the mists of time. Some churches still remember their founders in their dedications. St Nectan is the patron saint of Stoke Church, Hartland. He came, possibly from Wales, to this wild and lonely peninsula in fifth or sixth century and his hermitage is near the church. Instow and Morwenstowe are 'stows' or holy places of their founders John and Morwenna. Braunton Church, St Brannock also remembers its founder in the decorative roof bosses and bench ends. St Brannock was a Celtic holy man who had to set up a church on the spot where he would find a sow and her piglets - that spo was Braunton! Nearby, in Lee, the church has moved and taken with it the sixth century name 'Wardrede', possibly a composite name for the 'holy man near the beach'. St Petrock, another 6th century pilgrim from Cornwall, has given his name to eight Devon churches including Parracombe. *See 'Cornwall, Walks to Churches', page 81.*

The Saxons came to Devon in 7th century and established churches and monasteries. Little remains of their buildings; wattle and daub or wooden churches disintegrated. Some were burnt by invading Danes as at Lydford. The Benedictine monastery of Exeter was devastated in such a raid in 1003 and took 50 years to recover. In another 500 years Henry V111 destroyed all monasteries. Some Saxon stones are to be found in the walls of later buildings and even the occasional font has survived. The most satisfying survival from this period is underground in the southeast: a Saxon crypt was discovered in Sydbury in 1898. The Normans, who came to Sydbury chose to replace the Saxon chancel and threw all the rubble into the crypt where it has lain undisturbed for centuries. They would be amazed at our delight in the rubble they spurned. Sydbury also has the relic of a preaching cross, possibly left by monks in 6th century. Another Saxon find in the southeast is a cross that has been reassembled and displayed at Colyton. In the late 9th century King Alfred administered the towns of Devon. Exeter was one of his fortified burhs and had several Saxon churches. Bodelia, later Bodley was also a large royal domain. East Budleigh church has Saxon stones in one of its walls. The ecclesiastical centre of administration moved from Sherborne in 8th century to Crediton in the 10th century and finally to Exeter in 1050. St Boniface was born in Crediton in 680 and educated at the monastery in Exeter. He became a missionary to Germany. Saxon monasteries at Exeter, Tavistock, Buckfast, Hartland and Plympton have disappeared apart from the outlines of some foundations and the Abbey Chapel, Tavistock..

'Boniface, Aldhelm, Asser and Leofric were our founding fathers. They are men whom we can still get to know from their books. Boniface was a linguist and letter writer, Aldhelm a poet and scholar, Asser the biographer of King Alfred and Leofric a book collector. They remind us that, over 1000 years ago, Devon was not a backwater but home to leading scholars of the day.' – Canon Professor Nicholas Orme (The Pilgrim`s Guide to Devon`s Churches). He goes on to describe the development from minster churches in 900 A.D. to Parish churches in 1100 A.D.

The Normans The long arm of William the Conqueror stretched into Devon, replacing churches and cathedrals, taking over monasteries and establishing new ones. He gave land and positions of authority to his supporters, the men who had fought with him in 1066. They determined to show the Saxons how it should be done. Using mainly local stone, they built solid churches, simple nave and chancel or some of them cruciform. The chancel at the east end was the domain of the priest with his stone altar. The nave was larger and lacked seats; the standing or kneeling congregation had to peer the length of the church and listen to the Latin service. By 1287 seats were available in Devon`s churches. The windows were small and the doorways placed on the south side. A few churches have kept this shape - West Down and West Ogwell.

More often, the Norman church has been incorporated into a larger medieval one.

Some churches have Norman pillars or strong towers from that period. Crediton, an early cathedral, retains its Norman tower and crossing, also its Lady Chapel and south vestry. Bishopsteignton has a fine portal with colonettes and zigzag carving. It also has a tympanum as does Bondleigh. St Petrox at the mouth of the River Dart was first a chapel having a light to guide ships. The south aisle of that church is probably the extent of the Norman building. Salcombe Regis retains a Norman pillar, some stonework and a font. Branscombe has a square Norman tower with carved corbels on the outside. Other towers are at Otterton, Cockington and South Brent. Rattery`s tower is less impressive but the rare Norman font of red sandstone has a bowl with shallow flutings. A similar font is at Dittisham. There are 12 girdle fonts in Devon, for example one at Harberton. It has a carved girdle, shaped like a rope, around the middle. The most ornate of all the fonts is at Lupitt. There are 100 Norman fonts in Devon.

Perhaps the finest Norman work in Devon is in Exeter Cathedral. The medieval builders retained the two fine square Norman towers above the transepts. Churches built on Norman foundations include Axminster, Shute, Colyton, Kentisbeare, Mortehoe and Tawstock. Clyst Hydon has kept a Norman name; the 'de Hidon' family founded this church.

The Medieval Church

In 12th century Bishop Bartholomew organised parishes around a mother church and dependent chapelries. Many churches were built in 12th and 13th centuries but parishes were large and worshippers had a long trek. Some estate owners applied to bishops for permission to build chapels or oratories attached to their homes. In 13 08 Sir Simon de Montecute was the first to build an oratory in his manor, La More, Lupitt. Other domestic chapels followed. By the end of 14th century most major houses had a private chapel.

In 14th century there was much rebuilding but this has been obscured by the golden age of Devon Churches in 15th and 16th centuries. Devonshire came into its own, spending its wealth on enlarging and beautifying its churches. Skilled wood and stone carvers set to work. The arch separating nave and chancel was widened or opened completely. They filled in the space with intricately carved screens, each one a work of art. A canopy over the screen had a gallery above it. A slim stone staircase at the side led up to the gallery. A large statue of Christ high in the centre was known as the 'rood'. For more on the 15th century and later, see 'Devon Church Walks - South and West'.

4 Walks near Ilfracombe

Walk 1: Ilfracombe, The Torrs, Lantern Hill (extension to Berrynarbor)

After a walk high on Torrs Park, descend to the Parish Church, then down to the Harbour where a chapel perched on a rock acts as a lighthouse. Extend the walk to Berrynarbor, seaside at Hele and return along the Torrs.

Starting Point: The National Trust Car Park for the Torrs   **GR**511474
Map: Ordnance Survey OL9   **Distances:**   1½ Miles in Ilfracombe
                                                    + 8 Miles lanes to Berrynarbor
Terrain: Hilly, coast and town with tarmac. Long Walk includes some cliffs
Local Information: 1. 'The Torrs' in west Ilfracombe are seven hills. The Victorians built select houses on the lower slopes, 'Torrs Park'
2. Chambercombe Manor in east Ilfracombe was the home of the Champernon family c. 1162 – 1562 and now attracts visitors as one of the most haunted houses in England. There are gardens and a tearoom to enjoy when the Manor opens, Good Friday to 31st October.   Phone 01271 862624
3. The village shop and post office in Berrynarbor is next to a free car park.

The Churches
Ilfracombe Parish Church, Holy Trinity is large and beautiful. The tower was built with thick walls around 900 to withstand Viking attacks. The site was perfect, on a spur of land between the two Wilder Brooks. Separate from the tower, the Norman

Ilfracombe

church stood on a probable Saxon site. Only the font remains from that period. When Bishop Stapleton of Exeter visited Ilfracombe in 1321, he declared the church was too small. So, the nave was lengthened, aisles were added and the tower was

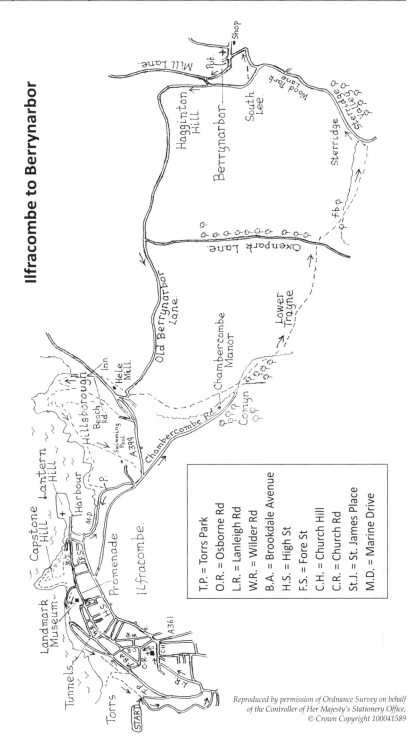

Ilfracombe to Berrynarbor

T.P. = Torrs Park
O.R. = Osborne Rd
L.R. = Lanleigh Rd
W.R. = Wilder Rd
B.A. = Brookdale Avenue
H.S. = High St
F.S. = Fore St
C.H. = Church Hill
C.R. = Church Rd
St.J. = St. James Place
M.D. = Marine Drive

*Reproduced by permission of Ordnance Survey on behalf
of the Controller of Her Majesty's Stationery Office,
© Crown Copyright 100041589*

incorporated in the north aisle. A corner has been cut away to allow a view of the altar. The plain octagonal pillars in the nave are 14th century. The shape of the present day church was established in 15th century. It was then that the chantry chapels were built and the Perpendicular windows inserted. They have a variety of fine Victorian stained glass. The east window is entirely Victorian as is most of the chancel. Only a medieval Piscina stands in the southeast corner. Besides fine windows, the church has handsome wagon roofs. In the nave the corbels are mythical beasts of 1321 and angels were placed above them, probably in 15th century. The chancel roof was replaced in 1899. It has 80 bosses carved by Margaret Down who also made the screens between chancel and aisles.

St Nicholas Chapel on Lantern Hill has long been a beacon guiding ships into the Harbour. From 1321 until the Dissolution of the Monasteries in 1540, it served as a chapel. It became home of the lighthouse man and his family 1835-71. Since then it was neglected and used as a reading room and laundry. It has now been restored by the town`s Rotarians and a few services are held here. The porch has become a small chancel. See the cover painting

St Peter`s Berrynarbor stands on the site of an early cruciform church. The north transept arch and the font base are Norman. The chancel is Early English with two small windows that may be earlier. The east window is Victorian. The handsome tower, 96 feet high was built in 15th century. The pinnacles are above corbels on the corners. There are six bells. Inside, the tower arch is a fine feature. The nave has a four-bay arcade to the south aisle, built around 1500, slightly later than the tower. The nave, chancel and aisle have modern oak cradle roofs. The porch roof with carved bosses is 16th century. The lych gate is 17th century.

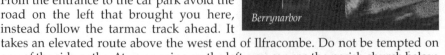

Berrynarbor

The Walk

From the entrance to the car park avoid the road on the left that brought you here, instead follow the tarmac track ahead. It takes an elevated route above the west end of Ilfracombe. Do not be tempted on any of the side paths. At an opening on the left, you can see the parish church below.

At the end of the tarmac track, you come down to a new housing estate in Langleigh. Turn left to leave the estate on Langleigh Road. Pass terraces of older houses then a side road, Trinity Gardens. Ahead, beyond the cemetery walls, you can see Trinity Church. Enter through the lych gate.

A path on the right takes you past the church and down to Brookdale Ave. Keep going to the next road. Turn down to Wilder Road. Pass the entrance to the Tunnels Beach on the left. Next you come to public parks and the Landmark Centre with café, tourist information, toilets and theatre.

You have reached sea level and continue on the promenade past Capstone Hill. Keep going along St James Place to the Harbour. Presiding over water, boats, shops and car park, the little, steep Lantern Hill has a chapel on top.

To continue from St Nicholas Chapel on Lantern Hill

*For the short seaside walk in Ilfracombe, return past the harbour shops to the Landmark Centre. Go to the nearby park and climb up to the top left hand corner. You join the Torrs Walk here and head back to the Car Park.

For the Long Walk to Berrynarbor, go to the head of the Harbour and turn left past the fish shop. Walk beside the quay. You are on Marine Drive Road. This road curves to the right. Avoid parks and parking on the left. You come up to the main A339. Cross diagonally left to Chambercombe Road. This heads southeast uphill past houses to become Chambercombe Lane.

Gardens and stream are below on the left. Tearooms are next to the Manor. Pass the Manor on your left and continue southeastwards on the enclosed lane. Avoid paths up in the woods on the right. You come to cottages at Comyn.

Cross to the far left corner to a bridleway over a stream.

Climb through Comyn Wood to elevated fields. At Lower Trayne Farm veer left then right. Pass the farm on the right and keep going uphill on the farm track to Slew Hill where you cross Oxenpark Lane.

Cross the lane to the footpath opposite where a new view opens to the north and animal tracks up the hill to the left. You veer to the right to the next field. Here you head for the strip of woodland on your right. Work your way down the edge of the field until you come to a finger post directing you into the trees. First you have a muddy patch, a stile and a footbridge to contend with. Maintain your course to emerge from the trees and keep to the right hand side of steeply sloping fields overlooking the lovely Sterridge Valley with scattered cottages. At the bottom the path swings left then right.

You are now on the valley road and turn left to Berrynarbor. Avoid the first turning to the right. At the second turning on the edge of the village, turn right for the Church.

As you approach the Church, note a lane on the right leading to the community shop

From Berrynarbor Church cross to the pub and pass it on your right. Walk down Pit Hill where at first you find the occasional shop. Just after the bridge over the stream, turn left to a T-junction.

If you prefer to return on footpaths and avoid the cliff coastal walk, turn left here back along Sterridge Valley and turn right to retrace your steps.

For the walk along lanes, turn right at the T-junction to join the cycle route up Hagginton Hill. In 1 mile pass Oxenpark Lane on the left and continue westwards on Old Berrynarbor Road. This brings you down to Hele.

At the edge of Hele, turn right just before crossroads. A track leads past the old mill, complete with water wheel, and on to the main road, A399. An inn is on the corner. Cross with care to Beach Road opposite. At Hele Beach the café is open in season. Pass toilets on the left and find steps in the nearby corner of the beach.

Follow the coast path as it swings back and forth over steep cliffs at Hillborough before a straight descent to Ilfracombe. The sea is on your right.

Return along Marine Drive to the Harbour. Follow instructions for the short walk above* to return to the car park on the Torrs.

Walk 2: Mortehoe to Lee

A switchback coastal walk, suitable for a fine day, returning through woodland and fields

Starting Point: The car park in Mortehoe (pay and display)   GR458453
Map: OS Explorer 139   **Terrain:** Steep coastal slopes, strenuous
Distance: 6 Miles. **Note:** Take your time on the Coast Path. Stop to enjoy the views and rest awhile. There are several seats.
Local Information: 1. Mortehoe is a small picturesque village of grey stone, above the hazardous cliffs where ships foundered and smugglers and wreckers operated. A Museum and Information Centre near the car park gives a history of the area. Now a popular tourist place, the village has shops, hotels, tearooms and pubs. Cheerful and chummy but quite unspoilt.
2. Lee is set in 'fuchsia valley' where one long lane leads through cottages to the rocky bay. We walk up this lane to the ancient pub and little church.

The Churches
St Mary`s, Mortehoe dominates a village mentioned in Domesday and popular today. The rectangular nave shows the extent of the Norman church, founded by

Mortehoe

William de Tracey in 1170. The tomb bearing his name in the south transept is probably not his. The round south doorway and the original entrance from tower to nave are Norman. The belfry and the chancel were added around 1275. The south and north transepts date from 1307 and 1500 respectively. A fine barrel roof and carved pews are typical features of a Devonshire church. There are bench end

Mortehoe to Lee

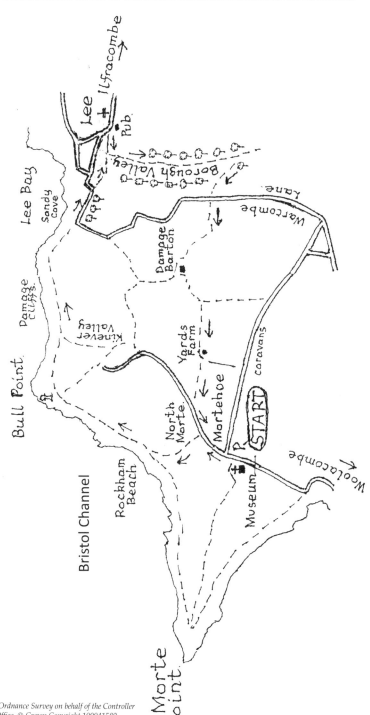

carvings of 30 pieces of silver, the robe, dice and a rod of hyssop. The Victorians also enhanced this church with the glass designed by Henry Holiday, fitted into the east windows of chancel and north aisle. The mosaic on the chancel arch by Selwyn Image was unveiled in 1905.

St Matthew and St Wardrede, Lee nestles into the side of the slope above this hamlet, as if it had been here since Domesday. It even has a dedication to a possible Celtic saint of 7th century. In fact the original St Wardrede`s Chapel is nearer the sea, its stones incorporated in Chapel Cottage. The illusion of great age is continued inside this church where carved oak panels, the pulpit, the front pews and pew ends all came from the old manor house. They are Jacobean, of 16th – 17th century. A small window, south in the chancel has a scene in old Italian enamelled glass of cattle being blessed. The chapel

Lee

walls have delightful paintings of Christian emblems. They are Victorian. The church was in fact built in 1834 in the reign of William 1V. The adjacent village school came over a decade later. It is now a charming gift shop.

The Walk

From Mortehoe Car Park go to the entrance and cross to the road opposite, North Morte Road. Pass the Post Office and continue for ¼ Mile to a footpath on the left. Turn left here towards Rockham Beach.

You are on an elevated path heading towards cliffs. The path curves to the right and down to the South West Coast Path with its acorn symbol. Turn right and follow a dramatic section of this long distance path for about 2 miles. *You have cliff views with the sea breaking on the rocks below and, in the distance behind, Lundy Island. On a clear day you can see the coast of South Wales ahead.*

Avoid the path down to Rockham Beach and also paths on the right leading back to Mortehoe. Instead, brace yourself for the steep climbs and descents of the Coast Path. At Bull Point you pass the lighthouse where cottages are now holiday lets. Continue past Bennet`s Mouth and Damage Hue Cliffs. At Sandy Cove you have the last climb up and along to Warcombe Lane.

At this narrow tarmac road turn left and walk down to Lee foreshore. At the car park turn right and follow the enclosed twitten past toilets to the village. ¼ mile into this path, just before the village road, you pass a **footpath** on the right towards woodland. This is our return route.

For now, continue on the twitten to Lee Village Road. Turn right to the nearby pub, 'the Grampus'. The little village church is nearby up on the left among pretty cottages.

From Lee Church return to the footpath, now on your left and head for Borough Woods. Inside the wood, the path forks. *The right fork leads up behind a large house and across to Warcombe Lane.* I have chosen the left fork, heading due south along Borough Valley and following the stream on the left for one mile, mostly muddy!

When the trees begin to thin and you can see light ahead, turn right. A steep path rises above the way you have just come and takes you up through trees, bears left and out of the woodland at last.

The way ahead, northeast across fields, is clear. First you have to cross Warcombe Lane again, with the aid of tall stiles facing each other in the hedges. You are about 1 mile south of the Coast Path and can look across to the cliffs. The path becomes a track through gorse and scrub. In ¼ mile, as you approach unsightly sheds in a dip, turn left down to Damage Barton. The walls of this 16th century building are on your left and vegetable gardens on your right.

Follow the driveway passing in front of the old farm and climbing out of the dip. Rest a while on a seat given by appreciative visitors for us to enjoy the views to the coast. Leave the driveway as it bends to the left and turn right onto a footpath heading east in the lea of a hedge on the right.

You come to Yarde Farm and turn left to pass the holiday homes and shop. Keep straight on at the caravan site and you come out at a higher point on North Morte Road. *The entrance to the access track to Bull Point lighthouse is on your right.*

Turn left and walk down the road past holiday flats and local houses and the familiar Rockham Beach footpath on the right. When you reach the end of North Morte Road, cross to the car park opposite.

Walk 3: Combe Martin to Trentishoe

From the grandest church climb to Exmoor to the smallest church, returning on the dramatic cliffs of the Coast Path.

Starting Point: St Peter Ad Vincula, Combe Martin   **GR**587464   **Map:** OL9
Terrain: Very steep slopes, open road, coastal cliffs   **Distance:** 12 Miles
Local Information: 1. Combe Martin has south facing slopes, once favouring strawberry and vegetable crops. Its very long High Street is now popular with artists, tourists and motor cars.
2. Great Hangman 320 m. is the highest point on the South West Coast Path.
Note: The quickest and simplest way to Trentishoe is along open elevated Exmoor roads with grass verges. For walkers who prefer a traffic free route, the Coast Path is nearby. Allow plenty of time for steep cliffs.

The Churches
St Peter Ad Vincula, Combe Martin stands mid-way on the longest village street.

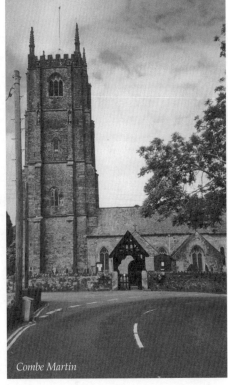

Built on the site of a Saxon church, the present building dates from the late 12th century. The tower, 99 feet high was completed in 1350. It has tall thin pinnacles, two tiers of gargoyles, battlements and large openings for 8 bells. Inside, the west door is Norman. The chancel has Early English windows. The Lady Chapel was added in 1333 for the priest to pray for the souls of the Columbers family and for King Edward 11. Remarkable features of this church include the screens. We can admire the finely carved parclose screen and the rood screen with Tudor paintings of Jesus and the Apostles. Harder to find are the two green men. Medieval wall paintings are near the font of 1427.

St Peter, Trentishoe a tiny remote church has grown into the hill that shelters it. This is the ideal place for pilgrims on foot. Few people live here. The clear glass windows look out on Exmoor. Despite the sense that the first church here from ancient times has

Combe Martin

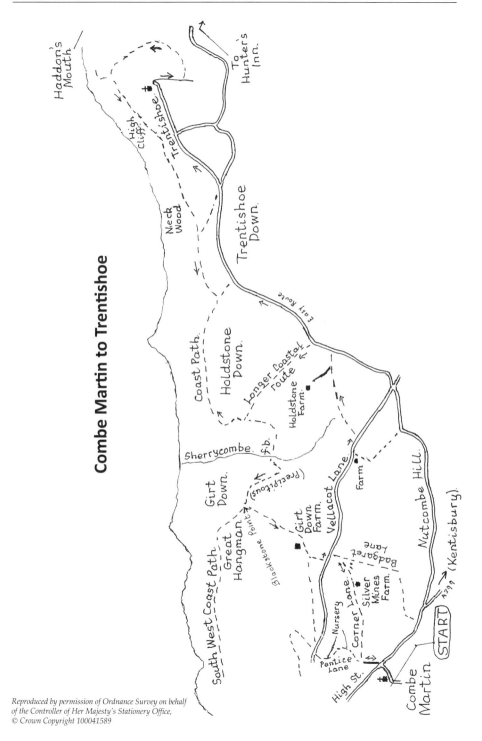

Combe Martin to Trentishoe

Trentishoe

changed little, I read that the little tower was rebuilt in 1638 and the chancel was enlarged in 1861. The musician`s gallery still has its hole for the bow of the viol.

The Walk

Sections in italics give an alternative coastal walk.

From Combe Martin Church, cross the main road to Corner Lane opposite. Start Climbing! In 250 metres Corner Lane bends to the right. Occasional glimpses through the hedges give views over the church to the countryside behind. You are heading east then northeast. In about 1 mile you pass a farm and then the chimney of an old silver mine. You soon come to a T-junction Turn left to another T-junction. Here a tarmac road runs high above the Combe to the south with the edge of Exmoor to the north. This is Vellacot Lane. *For the Coast Path turn left then immediately right into Girt Lane. Climb for 1 Kilometre nearly to the summit of Great Hangman. Turn right to follow the wall on the right and then a precipitous drop into Sherrycombe.* **For the easy route,** turn right and walk for 1 kilometre along this top road. Shortly after passing Vellacot Farm on the right, turn left into a footpath across fields. Go through the middle of the first field. Then follow the hedge on the left through 3 fields to join a driveway. Holdstone Farm is to the left. Turn right away from the farm. You come to a high Exmoor road. Turn left.

For the Coast Path turn left again in ¼ mile at a sign to 'Holdstone Down'. This path goes through trees at first but it is easier to walk on a bumpy bank. Then follow the farm wall on the left and heath on the right. You are on the lower slopes of Holdstone Down. The clear track bends left, still beside the wall then curves to the right to join the Coast Path. A finger post shows Combe Martin to the left and Hunter`s Inn (beyond Trentishoe) to the right.

For the easy route, continue on the high Exmoor Road northeast for 1 mile to a junction. Fork left on the Trentishoe Lane, remote and lovely. You have fine views to fields and moorland but beware the odd car! In another mile you come down to Trentishoe Church on a bend.

From Trentishoe Church continue on the lane that swings to the right and sinks steeply downhill passing only one or two cottages. In ¼ mile turn left into a grassy footpath. It follows a shelf around the hill, high above Hunter`s Inn, then curving northwards so that you look down on the valley leading to Heddon`s Mouth.

In 1 mile you come to the Coast Path. *This is now our only route west. If you should wish to rejoin the road, take one of the escape paths to the left.*

Turn left and enjoy walking on the gentle slopes above the sea with dramatic cliff views. In over 1 mile the Coast Path curves inland to avoid a cleft in the cliff and climbs around Holdstone Down. In ½ mile the Coast Path veers inland again then descends a steep slope to Sherrycombe. Cross the footbridge over the fast flowing brook. Great Hangman looms ahead.

On the other side of the brook, veer left towards trees then sharp right up a narrow precipitous path. You look down on Sherrycombe, the abode of sheep and shrubs. When you finally reach the top, follow the wall on the left to Blackstone Point and a fingerpost. You leave the Coast Path here.

*The summit of Great Hangman is ¼ mile away in the Combe Martin direction (**not** our end of that village).*

To return to Combe Martin Church turn left to 'County Road' and head southwest. Go down the field slope to pass a barn and join Girt Lane. Keep on course. In one kilometre from Blackstone Point, you come to habitations. Soon after Girt Down Farm, avoid a turning to the right and reach Vellacot Lane again. Turn left. In 100 metres you come to the familiar Corner Lane. Turn right and retrace your steps down to Combe Martin Church.

Walk 4: Braunton to Marwood

This is an inland walk over fields, tracks and through woods to find two ancient churches, a lovely garden and, maybe, a ruined chapel on a hill.

Starting Point: St Brannock`s Church, Braunton   **GR**489371
Map: OS Explorer 139 **Terrain:** Gentle hills and valleys   **Distance:** 9 Miles
Local Information: Marwood Hill Gardens, open 1st March – 31st October and occasionally in winter. Free entry to Tea Rooms Phone 01271 342528
Note: A separate summer route, when the ground should be dry, is in small print.

The Churches
The Church of St Brannock, Braunton. St Brannock was a Celtic holy man who

Braunton

sailed from Wales up the Taw Estuary to land at Braunton Burrows in 6th century. According to legend, he had been told to build a church on the spot where a sow had her young. This famous sow and other legendary characters are portrayed in the bench ends inside the church. The nave is full of chestnut seats with carved bench ends that date from 1500 to 1600. Carvings depict saints, including St Brannock, stag heads and his cow. The wide Perpendicular wagon roof of the nave has some interesting bosses. One of a sow feeding her young is above the font. A rood screen separates the nave from the chancel, covering the arch. The lancet windows on both sides of the chancel are original. The Victorians restored the damaged Perpendicular east window and filled it with stained glass. There is a contemporary description of the glass before it was destroyed by Puritans. It contained legends linked with St Brannock. The south aisle has Tudor arches. There are two transepts. The north transept has a gallery with Jacobean woodwork. The south transept is formed by the lower part of the tower. It has a Saxon tomb on the lintel of the west window. The broach spire may be the oldest in Devon.

St Michael`s Chapel on the hill looks out to sea. The people of Braunton would pray for sailors and fishermen here. This Perpendicular chapel is so well built that the landowner was physically unable to demolish it in 1790!

Braunton to Marwood

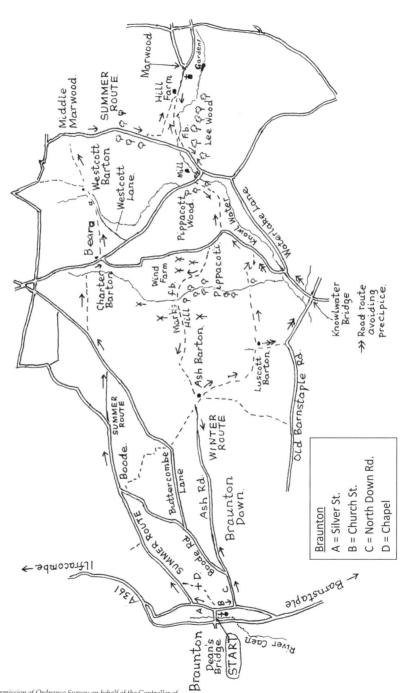

Braunton
A = Silver St.
B = Church St.
C = North Down Rd.
D = Chapel

St Michael's Chapel ruin, Braunton

Marwood

St Michael and All Angels, Marwood is a retiring rustic building with unsealed wagon roofs. The 13th century chancel retains its piscina of that period. The chancel was remodelled in 14th century. The rest of the church; nave, tower, north aisle and south chapel is mainly 15th century. The tower in three stages has a turret and battlements. The south porch also has battlements. The 5 bay arcade between nave and aisle is Perpendicular with flower and leaf capitals. There is a fine screen, given by Sir John Beaupel, parson 1520. It stretched across the church but was sawn off in 1850 so that only a section is left. Carved bench ends are in the nave. Colourful glass was fitted to the east window and the tiny transept window in 1910. The sundial by John Berry (1762) on the south porch tells the time in Europe and Jerusalem.

The Walk

From Braunton

SUMMER ROUTE - *(describes possible summer route to the Chapel and Marwood).*

From Church Street head north and cross to Silver Street. Bear right to climb Chapel Hill. Access to St Michael`s Chapel is on the right. Continue northeast along the farm track hemmed in by hedges and covered in slurry in winter. In 1 mile you reach the farming hamlet of Boode.

Turn left on the Boode Road. In ¼ mile, turn right into a track where a deep puddle welcomes you and keep on course eastwards. At a T-junction turn left to walk along Buttercombe Lane for ¼ mile. Turn right to continue eastwards along a footpath for nearly ½ mile to Beara.

Pass ancient Beara Barton on the right. Turn right to walk down past farms to a fork in the road. Take the left fork and turn immediately left into a farm track. *There is no footpath sign and, I think, most walkers probably go down to a second turning, Westcott Lane.*

If you brave the first turning, follow the hedge on the left. The path veers left and goes through scrub land on the hill slope and down to Knowl Water. Cross this stream on a footbridge and join Westcott Lane to pass the buildings of Westcott Barton on the left.

Westcott Barton

When you come to an old stone barn with a tiled roof, choose carefully:

For the field route turn right. Go through a rickety gate into a field. Follow the hedge on the left.

Survey the next field with care before entering to make sure there are no angry bullocks.

For the road route, *if you find livestock here, return to the barn and turn right to continue on the track up towards Beara Down. Turn right on the top road and right again at Middle Marwood.*

If you choose the field route it is a short distance straight across to the stile opposite. Steep steps on the other side of the stile bring you down into a dark leafy track. Follow this to nearby Middle Marwood and turn right.

Both routes, head south on the road through this pretty hamlet. The road passes through countryside with a stream on the right. Avoid the first path on the left. In ½ mile from the hamlet, turn left into a meadow. The path follows the hedge beside the road on the right then swings left past trees and uphill. At the top you have a good view to Marwood Church ahead. You are heading southeast on an elevated path. Come down to Hill Farm then up the concrete lane to the church.

Marwood Hill Gardens is just a little further along the lane.

YEAR ROUND ROUTE from Braunton to Marwood is along Ash Road. *(Describes year round route to Marwood excluding the chapel).*

From the Start, go south along Church Street and look for a twitten on the left into North Down Road. Turn left and walk through housing for ¼ mile. At a fork in the road, avoid Boode Road on the left. Instead, take the right fork, Ash Road. It leads you up out of houses into the countryside. In 1 mile you reach the Manor House, Ash Barton.

Pass the 17th century manor house and turn right. You walk between the house and a barn. At the back of the house there are two footpaths, not immediately obvious. Avoid the path on the right in a covered lane. Instead, go straight on to a pond. Cross a narrow bridge over the pond to a new kissing gate into a field. Walk diagonally right, southeast across the field. *If there is a crop, you may have to walk around the edge on the right.* You come to another kissing gate into a large open field with extensive views. Keep on course *or once again go round the outside edge on the right.*

In the next sloping field you have a view to Luscott Barton below. Head towards this farming hamlet. Turn right at a muddy lane to the farm. *Avoid the footpath on the left beside the farm. It leads to a dangerous precipice and river crossing with no apparent bridge (I have reported to Devon C C).* Instead, go straight on down the lane past cottages. In ¼ mile at Old Barnstaple Road, turn left and walk down to Knowlwater Bridge. Turn left at crossroads into Waterlake Road. *You can follow this lane for over 1 mile, passing a road on the right and one on the left.*

The quieter, steeper way is to turn left in ¼ mile again. Here a narrow lane leads steeply uphill.

In 1 kilometre you come to a sharp bend in the lane. This is the centre of the tiny hamlet of Pippacott. Turn right into a track past cottages to a pleasant tree-lined way with views over Knowl Water. You enter Pippacott Wood and follow the footpath down to a byway. Turn right.

Pass Whitehall Mill on the left and you come to a T-junction. Turn left on the narrow lane ensconced in woodland. In ¼ mile take a footpath in the hedge on the right. It leads northeast around the edge of a hill then down to a footbridge on the left. Cross the stream and veer right to walk above the stream and into the hamlet of Marwood. The church tower can be seen ahead. A concrete drive leads up to the church and on to Marwood Gardens.

From Marwood Church (both routes) return down the concrete lane to Hill Farm. Follow the middle path across the field (you have already come this way unless you chose the summer route). Cross the footbridge over the stream on the left. On the other side, keep on course, southwest, walking around the slope of the hill. Lee Wood is up on the left. Woodland is also on the right. Find a stile in the hedge on the right and step into the Middle Marwood road at a lower point.

Turn left to walk along the narrow road for ¼ mile. At a road junction turn right and pass Whitehall Mill on the corner. You take a few steps along this new lane looking for a footpath in woodland on the left. (It may be familiar).

Follow the path up the hill slope through Pippacott Wood. Emerge to a pleasant tree-lined way with glimpses south over Knowl Water. This path leads to the little hamlet of Pippacott at cottages on a road corner. Turn right to walk up the road. Shortly after passing the entrance to Branch Farm, turn left just before a farm gate.

You are heading northwest along an enclosed farm track towards wind turbines.

In ¼ mile you reach woodland and veer right down to a valley with apple trees. On the fields above, wind turbines are scattered around. You come down to a stream among trees. Cross the footbridge to a way ahead through trees on Mark`s Hill. Head due west on the designated path through the turbines and keep on course to a track overhung with branches. Pass a barn on the left. You soon come to the lane to Ash Barton. Pass the manor house on the left and keep going on Ash Road to Braunton. At the end, you come to North Down Road and finally turn right to Church Street.

4 Walks near Barnstaple

Walk 5: Barnstaple to Tawstock

A riverside walk from a regional capital to a hidden backwater holding in surprise an enchanted cathedral-like church

Note: It was impossible to make this a completely circular walk - not enough bridges over the river - but you can change routes on your return, adding another mile. (Walkers from the station return via Barnstaple. Walkers from Barnstaple return via the station).

Starting Points: Barnstaple, St Peter and St Paul   **GR**558333 or
Barnstaple Station   **GR**555326   **Map:** OS Explorer 139
Terrain: Mainly flat riverside, a slight scramble where a stream joins the River Taw, undulating near Tawstock.   **Distance:** 6 Miles
Local Information: Barnstaple grew from its Saxon origins to be a port, a harbour and the main town of North Devon. Its bridge of 16 arches was famous from medieval times. In 19th century the river silted up and trade headed for its rival, Bideford. Barnstaple still holds a panier market.
Barnstaple Museum (01271 346747) has many varied exhibits and events.
   Tawstock Court was the seat of the Earls of Bath. The gatehouse, passed on our walk is all that remains of the original 15th century mansion that burnt down in 1787. Sir Bourchier Wrey built the present house. It has been a school and is now a private house again.

The Churches
St Peter`s Church, Tawstock makes a startling impact on a modest walk. Where you least expect it, this magnificent church comes into view just below the lawns of Tawstack Court. Despite this low position, the church inspires awe with its perfection, its size and tall central tower. Walk down the enchanted drive to the Lych Gate and 17th century porch with sundial by local craftsman, John Berry. Most of the church was built around 1340 when the Norman nave was enlarged by creating arches in the outer walls. The building, including the three-stage tower is of local stone. The arches in the tower form an unusual pattern. The south transept has a fine Italian plaster ceiling. The nave, chancel and chancel aisle have open timber wagon roofs. The Lords of the Manor at Tawstock were the Earls of Bath. William Bourchier was the first. The Wreys succeeded the Bourchiers in 17th century and have taken over the south transept. Fine tombs and memorials take up much space in the chancel, the chancel aisle, and the transepts. For more details, purchase the history and guide on sale in the Church. The dead inhabit this church, but if you want to view the wooden effigy of a 14th century lady who stood in a recess in the north wall of the chancel, you will have to call in at the Museum of Barnstaple.

Barnstaple to Tawstock

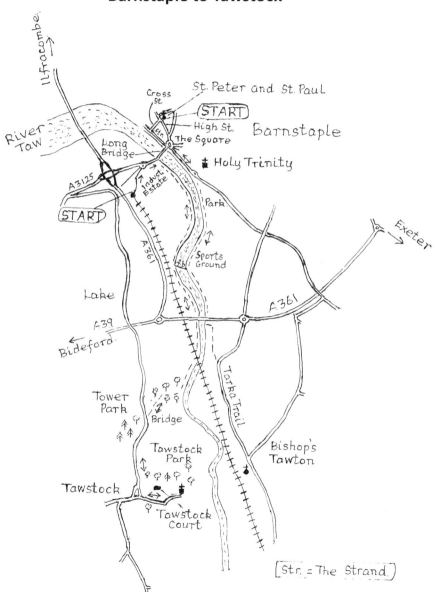

Tawstock

The greatest memorial is in the masonry and woodwork. The nave arches, the west window, the south Transept window and, later the chancel window are Decorated in style. The south aisle has Perpendicular windows. The chancel aisle was added in 16th century and has two square headed Tudor windows. The chancel screen, early 16th century is light and graceful. There are four 16th century benches with carved ends in the crossing. I will give due attention to the carving of Hinky Punk, as he has a habit of leading travellers into swamps, not a fate to be relished by a rambler!

Barnstaple, St Peter and St Mary Magdalene was built in 1318. The tower was added 1388-9 and stands where one would expect a transept. It has a broached spire covered in lead. The spire has developed a twist over the centuries. The arcades were rebuilt in 14th century. The church was originally cruciform and became rectangular when Perpendicular aisles were added. One window in the north chancel chapel is original Perpendiclar. Despite a thorough restoration in 1866 – 1880, the church has retained its medieval character. It shares this central site with **St Anne`s**, a 14th century chantry chapel, with crypt, now home of the Tourist Information Office.

Barnstaple, Holy Trinity supplies the skyline with a tall impressive tower in the Somerset style. It is slightly shorter than when built in 1842. In 1867 the Victorians decided to make a better job and rebuilt the whole church with arch-braced roof, apsidal chancel and slightly lower tower.

St. Anne's, Barnstaple

St. Peter's, Barnstaple

The Walk

From St Peter and St Mary Magdalene go over the High Street to walk along Cross St and on to the Strand. Turn left and walk beside the River Taw. Pass the Square and Tourist Information Centre to Taw Vale and follow Tarka Trail.

Trinity church can be seen on the left. From Trinity Church go to nearby Rock Park. Cross this park to return to the River Taw. Turn left to walk along Ladies Mile, also part of Tarka Trail. It is a wide tarmac walkway, shaded by various trees. In ¼ mile you pass a sports ground on the left. Stop when you come to steps up to a bridge.

Leave the Tarka Trail here and climb up to cross the old railway bridge over the river. You have views upstream back to the cityscape of Barnstaple.

Once across, turn right to descend the

Holy Trinity, Barnstaple

grassy slope then turn right again to go under the same bridge. ***Walkers from the station join here.*** *They have found their way through Seven Brethren Industrial Estate to the river where they turned right to walk along Macmillan Way West. In 1 mile they reached the old railway bridge to go under it.*

Both routes walk on a bank beside reed beds with the river on your left. In ½ mile go under the A39. In another ¼ mile go under the railway bridge carrying trains to and from Barnstaple.

Houses of Bishop`s Tawton can be seen across the river.

In another ¼ mile you come to the wooded slopes above a stream.

The stream, sliding down a waterfall, enters the river here.

Climb up the rough slope to a path above the stream. Look down on the old path strewn with fallen trees. In over ¼ mile you come to the lane to Tawstock. Turn left to cross rustic Shorleigh Bridge over the stream and continue along the lane. In this damp terrain it is good to have tarmac under foot. The lane goes under a bridge in Tawstock Park and climbs the wooded slope. In 1 kilometre you come to the first cottages in Tawstock.

Turn left at the sign to the church. This is an estate road and you go under a portico guarded with stone dogs. Pass old saw mills, a nursery school, then the old gatehouse and finally Tawstock Court that overlooks the church. Walk down this magnificent slope to Tawstock Church.

If you wish to vary the return walk, go back to the bridge with the asterisk. Walkers from Barnstaple continue on the left bank to the station. *Those from the station cross over the bridge and turn left to Barnstaple. To* get back to your starting place, you then have to cross the medieval Long Bridge.

Barnstaple

Walk 6: Arlington to Loxhore

Most of this walk is through woods and fields in National Trust land from a large estate building to a little church at the edge of a quiet hamlet.

Starting Point: The National Trust Car Park of Arlington Court **GR**614407 **Map:** OL9   **Terrain:** Partly estate walk, partly quiet lanes, gentle hills **Distance:** 5 Miles **Local Information:** Arlington estate was acquired in 1384 by the Chichester family when John Chichester married Thomasine Raleigh. Richard Chichester had been Bishop of Exeter 1138 –1155. The old manor house has been demolished and the present building re-sited in 1820. In 1830 John Chichester created a lake by damming the River Yeo. Miss Rosalie Chichester bequeathed the estate to the National Trust. She died in 1949. The grounds are open all year round. The house, shop and tearooms are open mid-March to end of October and some days throughout most of the year, **Phone** 01271 850296 for more details of **Arlington Court**.

The Churches
St James, Arlington was rebuilt in 1846 when Rev. J.H.J. Chichester was incumbent. In 1793 the Chichester family closed their Roman Catholic chaplaincy. The tomb in

Arlington

photo by Lobsterthermidor

Arlington to Loxhore

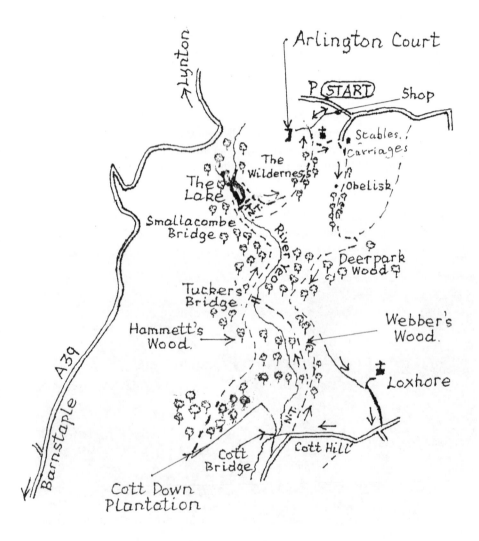

a recess in the chancel is 14th century. The robed effigy is likely to be that of Thomasine Raleigh. Her head is on a cushion supported by angels, her feet on a dog. There are other monuments to the Chichester family. The windows in this huge barn of a church have Perpendicular tracery. The stained glass of the east window is by Henry Halliday, 1885. The handsome west tower was added in 1899 and may have been similar to that of the original church.

St Michael and All Angels, Loxhore stands at the end of a quiet lane next to a pretty farmhouse. The church is small and quaint with wooden piers between nave

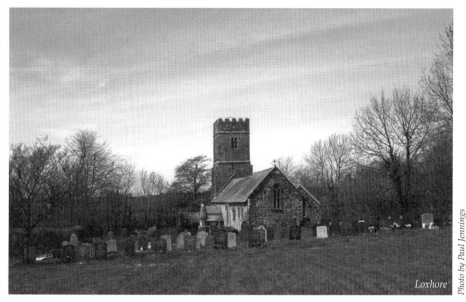

Loxhore

Photo by Paul Jennings

and the north arcade. The wagon roof has flower and leaf bosses. The chancel has a kingpost roof with four-way struts. The narrow windows in the chancel are unusual. The east window remembers James Chichester who was rector here and at Arlington for 60 years. The west tower has six bells, rung from the tower floor. The old font has a 16th century cover with cable ornament.

The Walk

As you enter the grounds of Arlington from the shop, the church is on your left among trees on the far side of the lawns.

After visiting Arlington Church, turn left and carry on along the drive past the Coach Museum. Large green arrows mark an estate walk that we follow for much of the way. Go through a small coppice to an open field. Turn sharp right to pick up another arrow.

Then turn left into a pleasant leafy walk heading south. On the right, note the obelisk, standing on the spot where a bonfire celebrated the Jubilee of Queen

Victoria in 1887.

In ½ mile, your enclosed path turns left then right into Deerpark Wood where oak, ash and beech trees grow. About 500 metres into the wood, you come to cross paths with a fingerpost.

The track on the left is marked to Loxhore Church. Follow this track as it veers up to the left heading southeast and out of the wood.

You now have to cross a field with only the aid of small arrows for this right of way. First keep fairly close to the edge of the wood on your right. The wood falls away and you stay on course to the field boundary. There is a hidden track in the corner where several fields meet. This enclosed track takes you southeastwards to the end of a lane. Turn left for Loxhore Church.

From Loxhore Church return down the lane, past the track that brought you here. There are remarkably few houses here. In ¼ mile you come to a bigger road and turn right. Walk downhill, keeping to the edge of the road and avoid two turnings to the left. In ½ mile the road bends left and there is a narrow lane straight ahead. **Stop here.**

Just past a large house on the right, look up to the two stone herons that adorn the entrance to the private driveway. Herons are on the crest of the Chichester family. Turn right into this drive, pass the house again and continue through the National Trust land.

An alternative route if you wish to follow only rights of way: you can continue on the narrow lane down to the River Yeo and follow the mapped path through Cott Down Plantation and Hammett`s Wood.

The driveway through National Trust land heads generally northwards through Webber`s Wood for a mile. *Look out for wood sorrel and ferns. The River Yeo is down on the left.* Avoid the track forking to the right to Deerpark Wood. Instead, follow signs to Arlington Lake. Cross the river at Tucker`s Bridge.

At the T-junction on the other side, turn right. You have joined the public right of way. The river is on your right. Pass Smallacombe Bridge (the right of way crosses here). Continue to the lake.

Turn right and pass the lake on your left. A footpath up on the right takes you back to Arlington Court via the wilderness.

Walk 7: Parracombe to Martinhoe

From a little gem, rescued for posterity, a fairly gentle climb brings you up to St Martin`s Church near the coast and lovely coastal woodland

Starting Point: Car Park near the recreation ground and toilets, Parracombe **GR**671450   **Map:** OS Explorer OL9   **Terrain:** Gentle field slopes, ford through a shallow stream, delve into Woody Bay as an optional extra   **Distance:** 7 Miles
Local Information: 1 mile of railway, run by volunteers is all that remains of the Lynton to Barnstaple line. Steam engines pass us as we walk on a permissive path.
Parracombe was an important centre with Manor and Haddon House. It was sidelined as the Victorians developed Lynton and Lynmouth in 1880s
Woody Bay resisted their efforts to commercialize it. A tarmac road still leads through trees to the bay but Benjamin Lake`s pier has collapsed.

The Churches

St Petroc`s Parracombe has retained its simple Georgian interior over 200 years. The church was rescued from demolition in 1879 thanks to the work and generosity of John Ruskin and friends. In 1908 the tower was repaired after damage by lightning. Further major repairs were needed in 1969. The Churches Conservation Trust took over the care of this lovely building in 1971. The chancel and lower part of tower are probably 13th century. Between the Perpendicular nave and the south aisle, the arcade of four bays has piers with leaf capitals; the arches are slightly depressed. An unusual gated screen separates the nave and chancel. On a massive tympanum above, one can read the Lord`s Prayer, the Creed and the Commandments. The seating and pulpit are typical of an 18th century village church. To complete the picture, there is plain glass in the windows, weathered

Parracombe

Parracombe to Martinhoe

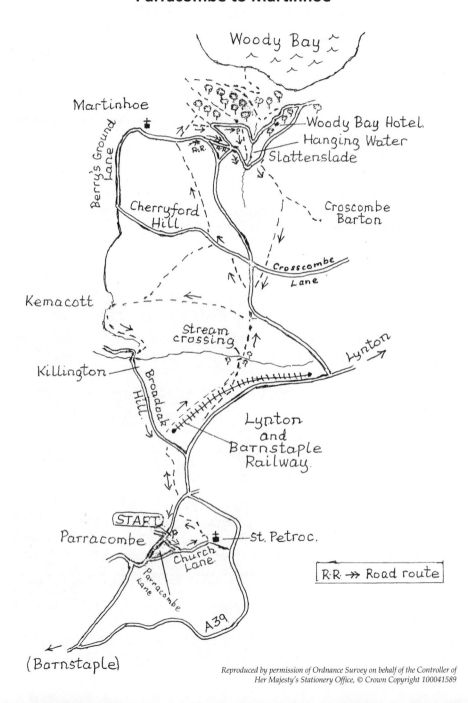

Woody Bay

Martinhoe

Woody Bay Hotel.
Hanging Water
Slattenslade

Berry's Ground Lane

R.R.

Cherryford Hill

Croscombe Barton

Crosscombe Lane

Kemacott

Stream crossing

Lynton

Killington

Broadaok Hill.

Lynton and Barnstaple Railway.

START

Parracombe

St. Petroc.

Church Lane.

Parracombe Lane

A39

| R.R. ⇒ Road route |

(Barnstaple)

Martinhoe

granite stones on the floor and wagon roofs with simple bosses.

St Martin`s, Martinhoe was originally a Saxon chapel above Woody Bay. The whole extent of it probably fitted into the chancel. The present chancel dates around 1300. Standing high above the north coast, the early church would have been a refuge for inhabitants fleeing from pirates. It was rebuilt in Norman times. The Norman font has been transferred to St Petroc`s, Parracombe. In its place there is a fine carved font of 1864. Much Victorian restoration has deprived the interior of this church of its ancient character.

The Walk

From the recreation ground head south along Parracombe Lane towards the Victorian church. Take the first turning left before you reach the church. You come to Church Lane. Proceed down this lane to St Petroc`s, the old church.

Facing St Petroc`s, follow the footpath on the left, northwest past Heddon Hall. At the end, Parracombe Lane forms a T-junction. Turn right. In 200 metres turn left into another path leading to Killington Lane Station.

Cross the road to the left of the railway line. Blue splodges on posts or trees mark the way of a permissive path beside the line. Head northeast along this path on the edge of fields on the left and enjoy the hill views. Passing trains on the right may shroud you in smoke occasionally.

In ½ mile veer left; a blue splodge shows the way through the hedge. Turn left away from the railway and follow the hedge on the left. You may have to steer around gorse. Suddenly, you come down to a cleft in the ground. A track leads down to the stream at the bottom. No-one has thought to put a footbridge here. In

October, it was shallow enough that our boots could cope

Continue up the other side, still hugging the hedge on the left. As you climb, turn to watch the trains behind.

In ¼ mile go through to the next field and turn right to walk to the **road**. Turn left and walk uphill. **A white finger post** up ahead is a road marker. Before you reach it, take the footpath on the left. It cuts across a corner of the field and brings you up to the lane to Mannacott. Turn left. In 250 metres turn right at a footpath sign to Woody Bay.

The path climbs gently up Cherryford Hill, following a tall beech hedge on the left. The hedge has been allowed to sprout into trees. In 1 kilometre you reach the top, oddly named, Berry`s Ground Lane. Turn left for nearby Martinhoe Church.

From Martinhoe Church retrace your steps to the path that brought you here. Just past this familiar turning, a path is on the left. You have a choice:

*For the diversion to Woody Bay turn left and walk down the narrow, sloping path. Avoid the turning on the left to Hunters Inn. Continue to join a road and head down past a **car park** under trees. The track on the left descends through woodland to Woody Bay.*

*Opposite, on the same side as the **car park** there is a narrow unsigned path. This is our way back. It climbs above a valley on the left and comes up to Berry`s Ground Lane. Turn left.*

2. For the short road route keep straight on along Berry`s Ground Lane. Head down to West Waters and Slattenslade.

Both Routes Follow the road down to cross 'Hanging Water' and take a sharp left turn. In 100 metres turn right into a footpath signed to 'Croscombe Barton'. The path takes you back above the road then turns left into a field.

Head southeast across fields, hugging the hedge on the left. At the fourth field, you come to a fingerpost on the left. Veer right and southwards to follow the direction to 'County Road'. You stay close to a Devon hedge on the left and look up across the wide field on the right. In 1 kilometre you come to Crosscombe Lane. **The same white finger** post is to the right now.

Go straight across to the gate opposite and down across the field to the familiar **road.** Turn left and go down to a sign on the right to Kemacott. Turn right and walk beside the fence on the left heading west for 1 kilometre

Below you may see the little steam trains chugging along.

As you approach Kemacott you join a farm track. In 200 metres turn left on the track down to Killington. Here, after curving to the right and crossing a stream, you come to the byway, Broadoak Hill. Turn left and walk with care down the hill to Killington Halt. Retrace your steps to the car park on Parracombe Lane.

Walk 8: Combe Park to Watersmeet, Countisbury Church and Brendon Church

Wild land between Exmoor and the Coast has leafy footpaths by rivulets of clear water. One church has been rebuilt and the other has been re-sited.

Starting Point: Combe Park National Trust Car Park off A39 and B3223   **GR**740477
Map: OS Explorer OL9
Terrain: Easy riverside on edge of steep hills. A climb to the coast and back
Distance: 6 Miles + 2 miles to extend the walk to Foreland Point
Local Information: Watersmeet was a lodge built by Rev. Walter Halliday, a friend of Coleridge and Wordsworth who enjoyed walking here. In 1934 the National Trust bought it and it has continued as a very popular tea house.
National Trust Exmoor Warden, Phone 01598 763306
Iron Age men lived in round houses in these hills. The ancient woods include rare whitebeams. Dartford warblers, whinchats, redstarts, stonechats and wheatears are listed in the National Trust handbook as breeding here.
*'(**Countisbury**) is a village on a hill, 1000 feet up, with the sea just out of sight over the top. The old coaching inn is still here.' – Arthur Mee*
Countisbury Inn, opposite the Church, is 300 + years old and still open to travellers and pilgrims. 6 horses pulled the coach up the hill from Lynmouth.
Warning: Rivers have been known to flood, so choose clement weather!

The Churches

Countisbury

Combe Park to Watersmeet, Countisbury Church and Brendon Church

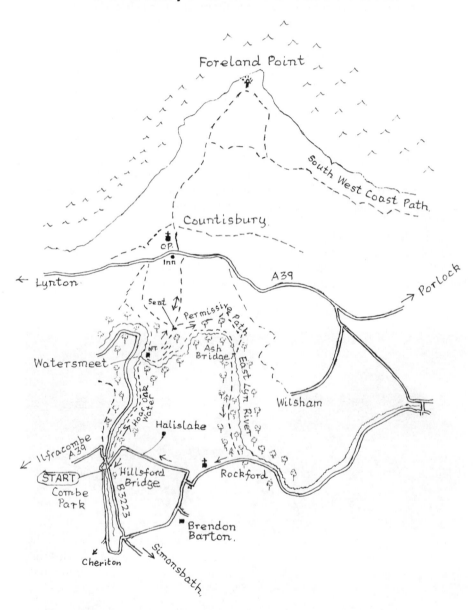

St John the Evangelist, Countisbury was built in 1796 on the site of an earlier church. This hilltop near Foreland Point was a lonely spot before the arrival of the Inn. The 18th century builders were local men who managed without an architect. The only medieval remnant is a carving of a crowned swan in the chancel south wall. In 1835 Rev. Halliday (see above) rebuilt much of the church, including the tower. It has obelisks on the corners at the top. Shipwrecked sailors are buried in the churchyard.

Parish Church of St Brendan, Brendon was originally built at Cheriton two miles away in 12th century. *If you wish to search for its base, head south from Combe Park Car Park.* The Bishop of Exeter pronounced it to be 'very frail and incommodious'. In 1738 Parishioners moved it stone by stone to this site, donated by the Chichester family. It consists of nave, chancel, tower and south porch. The sundial above the

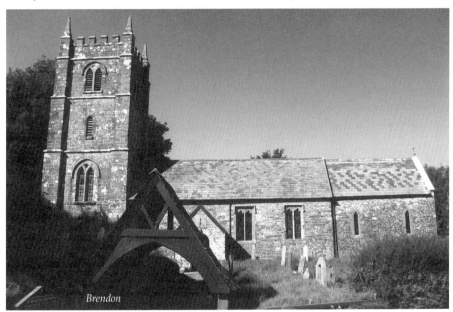

Brendon

porch dated 1709 and the Saxon font come from the earlier church. The tower was rebuilt in 1828 and has battlements. In 20th century local craftsman John Floyd made several fine carvings: the reredos, the choir stalls and the altar rails.

The Walk

Go to the car park entrance and turn right onto the B3223. Cross Hillsford Bridge over Hoar Oak Water and turn immediately left into the woodland path. This runs northwards above the water on your left. The path rises and descends under little beech and ash trees.

In 1 kilometre take the steps down to Watersmeet and cross to the café and shop, open in season. Turn right and pass this centre, keeping it on your left. Then turn immediately left into a footpath signed to 'Barton'.

This path heads east, rising above the East Lyn River. In 75 metres fork left into a path signed to 'Countisbury'. Begin the steep climb through little oak trees. There is a precipitous drop on the left. The path swings sharp left then right through the oaks. There is now a gentler climb up to a sheltered **seat** at crosspaths.

On the right of this seat, your path continues northwards over South Hill Common. You have a view over to Lynton on the left. Your path takes a **farm track** to the A39 at Countisbury (the main road has also climbed here).

The Old Coaching Inn is on your left. Cross the main road diagonally left to the Car Park opposite. Walk up the lane to the Church. *If you wish to go to Foreland Point and back, go behind the Church to join the Coast Path north*

From Countisbury Church return to the familiar farm track and retrace your steps to **the seat.**

Turn left to take the permissive path signed to 'Rockford'. This is a narrow gently sloping path down through Trilly Wood. In about ¼ mile avoid the turning to the left and continue down to East Lyn River. Turn left to the nearby Ash Bridge. *This footbridge has been designed to float in floods.*

Cross the bridge and turn left so that you are heading south with the river down on your left. This lonely stretch of woodland by the river is delightful with rocky pools and little waterfalls. In ½ mile you climb to a gate into a meadow. Go down to the road and turn right. (Rockford pub is to the left).

You are climbing away from Rockford up to the lonely Brendon Church. Pass the church on your right and continue uphill to Barton Cottages. The road bends to the right. At a T-junction turn right into a lane used as a cycle route. You have made a loop to Straypark Corner so that you are above the church. The cycle route takes an elevated course northwest with views to the coast. It then turns left down past woodland to the B3223 again.

Turn right for nearby Combe Park National Trust Car Park.

3 Walks near Bideford

Walk 9: Instow to Westleigh
Summer ferry to Appledore (Two hours either side of high tide)

A linear walk beside the Torridge Estuary and up to little hamlets, away from holiday makers then joining them on the sands.

Starting Point: Rectory Lane off B3233 **GR477311**   **Map:** OS Explorer 139
Terrain: Two short hills, sandy beach or Tarka Trail. **Distance:** 4 + Miles
Note: The rare opportunity to take the community ferry to Appledore from Instow Quay may add an extra mile to your walk
Tapeley Park was built around 1700 for William Cleveland, a naval officer. It has later extensions and was transformed 1898 – 1916 for Christie family.
Tarka Line, an old railway track from Exeter to Barnstaple and Ilfracombe, is now used by cyclists and walkers. It is part of Tarka Trail, 180 mile figure of eight. The name is from 'Tarka The Otter' a book by Henry Williamson.
Buses 21 and 21A run betw. Barnstaple and Bideford about every 20 mins

Churches
Instow Church, St John is on a raised circular graveyard, an early Celtic site. It has magnificent views over Bideford Bay. St John may have been brother of St Morwenna and St Nectan. Instow was 'Johannestow', meaning the 'stow' or holy place of John'. Today it is dedicated to St John the Baptist. All Celtic remains have blown away. The font is Norman. The chancel windows of circa 1300 have been

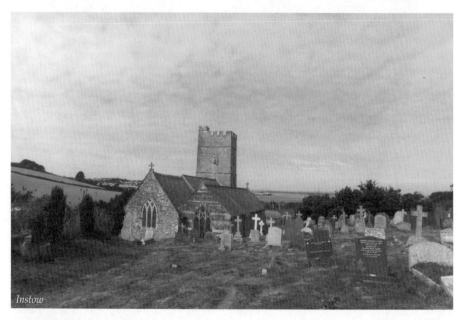

Instow

Instow to Westleigh
Seasonal ferry to Appledore

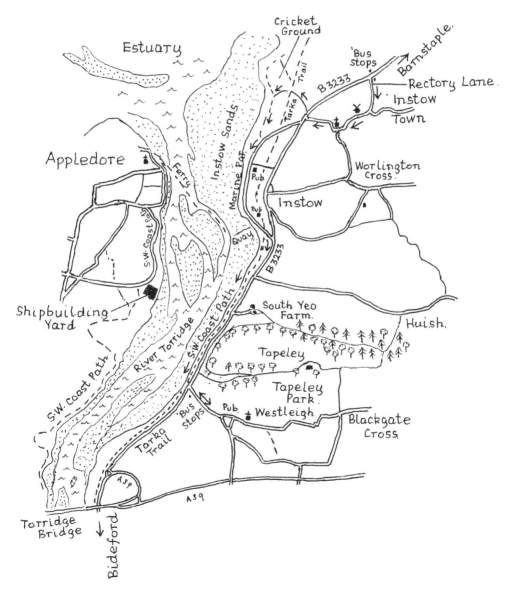

Instow

renewed. The north aisle of 1547 has a fine wagon roof. There is a dated inscription to Richard Waterman and his wife Emma on the capitals of two of the pillars. The carved oak screen, inserted in 1906, cuts across this arcade. Among the monuments is a memorial to the botanist, Humphrey Sibthorpe who died 1797. The battlemented tower has three stages and a turret.

Westleigh Church, St Peter has presided over many changes. In 13th century a fugitive claimed sanctuary in the Church of 'St Medom', Westleigh. Was Medom a Celtic saint? The Manor of Westleigh is mentioned in Domesday. It was held by Robert de Alberule. The Early English font incredibly holds 9 gallons of water. The oldest part of the church today dates from 1300. The chancel windows, designed then, have been renewed. The porch was added a little later,

It has good carved bosses probably taken from inside the church. The fine wagon roofs have bosses and angel figures on wallplates in the nave. Few surviving carved bench ends are in the nave. Some tiles are 15th century. The cruciform shape of the church changed around the year 1500, when the north aisle was added, absorbing the transept. The arcade has three bays and granite columns with bell capitals. The embattled 15th century tower has a stair turret. From the village the approach to the

Westleigh

church is through a building, reminding us of past life. In 1850 Westleigh Parish had 2 blacksmiths, 2 millers, 2 shoemakers, 3 masons, 3 carpenters, an innkeeper, a tailor, a shopkeeper, 2 butchers and 2 teachers at the National School, 1876 – 1981. Today, pretty residential cottages spread past the Inn to the Church.

Westleigh

The Walk
From the bus stop on the main road, walk up Rectory Lane to the top. Here you will find a handful of stone houses, 'Instow Town' the original centre.

Turn right and walk past the school to the Church. Continue down the lane, avoiding Worlington to the left, and you are back on the main road B3233.

Cross diagonally right to a footpath that runs beside a fenced MOD building. Escape over Tarka Trail and bear left to pass a cricket pitch and pavilion on the right. Rough paths or a track lead to the extensive sands of Torridge Estuary.

Turn left and walk over the sands to the more recent village of Instow. There are several pubs. A footpath beside the marine road leads you to the Quay. *There, if the tide is right, you can take a short trip to Appledore on the opposite bank of the river.*

Otherwise, follow the road as it bends left and passes a Post Office and well stocked shop. Almost immediately you are on Tarka Trail again. Just past the entrance to North Devon Sailing Club, turn right.

The Old Station platform has been converted into a picnic site with benches for cyclists and walkers on Tarka Trail. We join them on this tarmac track heading southwest for 1 mile, running parallel to the road on the left. It is a pleasant walk under the shade of trees at first. The River Torridge is on your right and the bridge carrying A39 can be seen ahead. Pass a stream bed at South Yeo Farm and trees that mark the boundary of Tapeley Park.

You can see Westleigh Church up on the left but cannot turn until you reach the official path leading to a bus shelter. Cross diagonally left to the road up to Westleigh, our second hill. As you reach the village, turn left and wend your way past the pub on a side turning, to the Church. If you continue on the lane past the Church you come to Blackgate Cross and Treyhill. Some locals go through the park.

Return to bus shelters on B3233 and await your transport. Stay this side for bus to Bideford or cross over for Barnstaple.

Walk 10: Hartland - Stoke Church to Hartland Abbey then on to Clovelly

A choice of walks on the rugged Hartland peninsula where Celtic saints brought early Christianity

Starting Point: Stoke Church Car Park on the road to Hartland Quay **GR**235246
Map: OS Explorer 126 **Terrain:** Hilly **Distances:** 4½ Miles + 7 miles to Brownsham and back + 2 Miles Brownsham to Clovelly
Return by bus, or energetic walkers may choose the Coast Path (17 Miles)
Local Information: This exposed Atlantic coast has been the scene of shipwrecks, wrecking and piracy. To provide safe harbour for fishing boats, quays were built at Clovelly in 14th century and Hartland 200 years later.
Hartland Abbey was first founded by the mother of the last Saxon king, Countess Gytha in gratitude to St Nectan for saving her husband from shipwreck. In 1169 Geoffrey de Dineham made it into an Augustinian abbey. After the Dissolution of the Monastries, it was given to William Abbott in1546. His descendants still own it. As a result of the changes they have made, the medieval building is quite lost. Admission to the gardens (Apr – Oct, 12 – 5 p.m.) also allows you to use the drive to **Blackpool Mill**, featured on TV`s 'Sense and Sensibility'.
Clovelly was a fishing village where the main street is on a steep slope down to the sea. Charles Kingsley lived here as a child and was inspired to write 'Westward Ho!' and 'The Water Babies'. There is a Kingsley Museum. In 20th century tourists discovered Clovelly and now pay an admission charge.
Phone 01237 431781
Clovelly Court just behind the Church, was seat of the Carys 1387 – 1795 then the Hamelyns 1795 – 1936. In 1929 Christine Hamelyn set up an estate company to look after the village.
Bus: 319 Stagecoach runs approx. every 2 hours between Bideford Quay, Clovelly Visitor Centre and Hartland. It connects with Bus 219 to Bude
This service is subsidised. Phone Traveline 0871 200 22 33

The Churches
The Parish Church of St Nectan, Stoke is a landmark on this bleak peninsula. The 14th century Perpendicular building stands on the site of a collegiate church founded around 1050. The ornately carved font is Norman, At the four corners the faces of the baptized look down on the faces of the unbaptized. 'Harton' was a royal manor in Saxon times. Before then St Nectan (5th – 6th Century) brought Christianity here. The Well near the church is thought to have been where he had a hermitage. How he would marvel at this grand church! The tower, in 4 stages with high pinnacles, is the tallest in North Devon and a marker for sailors. The four gargoyles and a statue of St Nectan on the east side are original. Inside, the tower arch is 8 metres high. The spacious nave has aisles with wide arches. The ancient pillars are of

Stoke Church to Hartland Abbey, then on to Clovelly

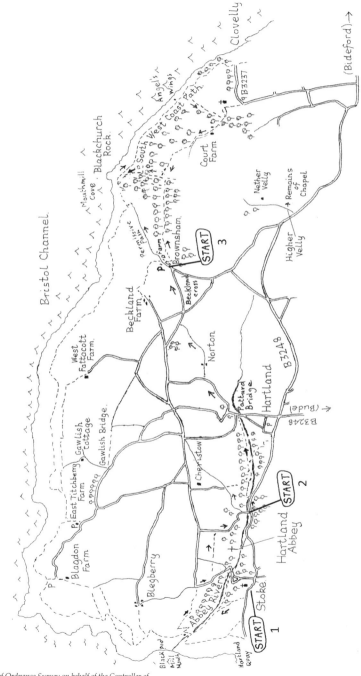

Photo courtesy of the North Devon AONB

Stoke

limestone. The wagon roofs are varied and interesting. In particular the Lady
Chapel on the north side of the chancel has original bosses. The fine oak screen is
14 metres long and 3 metres high. It is ornate and pure 15th century. The front coving
has 7 ribs with flowers and shields between the ribs. Coving at the back has 5 ribs.
The windows were renewed in 1848 and fitted with thick glass that has since been
mostly removed. Much plain glass now allows more light inside. The plain pews
are 18th century. Some in the south chancel chapel have carved bench ends, given
by Hugh Prust in 1530. A catacleuse stone tomb chest is on the north side of the
chancel. It probably came from Hartland Abbey after the Dissolution of the
Monasteries.

All Saints Church, Clovelly is ½ mile outside the village. A Norman church was
built here in 12th century. It was cruciform. The low west tower made from ashlar
has survived from that church. Norman features include the rounded tower arch
inside and the zigzag decoration on the south door. The church was enlarged in 14th
century. The north aisle was formed by first removing the north wall of the nave
and replacing it with an arcade of granite monoliths. The north transept became a
part of this aisle so the cruciform shape was lost and a Perpendicular style
introduced. In 1894 windows in the Decorated style were added. Both east and west
windows have glass by Charles Kempe. The north aisle has retained its original
wagon roof. The main wagon roof covers nave and chancel. The south porch was
added around 1450. It has a Norman doorway that had to be moved to the outside.

Clovelly

The porch also has a wagon roof and some original bosses. Monuments in the church remember lords of the manor. They have preserved the village and have also left their mark on the landscape.

The Walk
Part 1 *A circular walk from Stoke Church to Hartland Abbey (4½ Miles)*
From the Car Park continue along the lane towards Hartland Quay for just 250 metres. Turn right into a footpath that leads down past woodland and along a field boundary on the right. In 350 metres you come to the path beside tree-lined Abbey River. Turn left onto this path. The river is down on your right. In 1 kilometre enter trees and turn right at a path junction. Cross the little river and walk down to the pebbly beach at Blackpool Mill.

Walkers come down to this beach from cliffs on either side, walking on the South West Coast Path. Seats are on the grassy verge above the beach.

Reluctantly we turn inland on the driveway of a lone house (see above), Blackpool Mill. In 100 metres the driveway is private and we have to turn left. Here a steep narrow path leads up through bracken until you reach the cliff top. Turn right and keep going inland along elevated fields with views to the farm, Blegberry on the left and the tower of Stoke Church to the right.

In 300 metres you join an enclosed track, veering left. There were old caravans here when we passed through. The track comes to a T-junction. Turn right to wend your way on the tarmac lane past Berry Farm House. Then descend on the lane for 200 metres.

Turn left into fields where a footpath leads due eastwards. As you cross the grassy fields you look down on woods immediately below. Hartland Abbey is hidden in the trees. After the third field you come to a steep lane and turn right. Walk down through woodland for 300 metres to Hartland Abbey pedestrian entrance on the right.* *The lane leads down to Bow Bridge*

To visit the Abbey and return to Stoke, turn right to walk beside the drive then in front of the House. You pass the House on your right then turn left following another drive to the Exit gates. You are again on the road to Stoke. Turn right and climb the hill to the village and Stoke Church.

Part 2 Hartland Abbey to Brownsham (You can drive to Brownsham)
Starting Point: Bow Bridge   GR247247   **Distance:** 2 ½ Miles
Terrain: good path near the river, some lanes, one steep climb.
* Opposite the pedestrian entrance to Hartland Abbey turn into a footpath that runs through woodland. You are heading eastwards above the Abbey River on your right. In under ¼ mile climb slightly left, avoiding path to the right and keep on course. In ½ mile pass paths on left and right. Your eastward path is wider in a flat valley bordered by woodland.

In just over 1 mile from Hartland you come to Pattard Lane and turn left then immediately right. You have a steep hill to climb up to Norton Farm on your right. Turn right on the track through farm buildings. Come out through trees to open fields. Follow the hedge on the right until you reach a Lane.

Turn right to nearby crossroads, Beckland Cross. Then cross to the lane opposite. It leads through hedgerows to Brownsham.

Part 3 Brownsham Car Park to Clovelly
Starting Point: Brownsham National Trust Car Park, at end of narrow lanes
GR287259 Distance: 5 miles on recommended route **Terrain:** Gentle slopes, woodland, 1 steep climb, sea views

Pass the Car Park on your left following the rough access lane down to Lower Bransham Farm. Here the track on the right is signed to 'Mouthmill'. This is the route I took.

It is possible to turn left in front of the farm for a signpost to a permissive path to the coast. It is a more open route but involves precipitous cliffs.

I recommend you take the gentle slope through Brownsham Wood. The stony track curves down behind the farm and is joined by a stream. *Butterflies benefit from the shelter and flutter over the Meadow Sweet and Hemp Agrimony in summer.*

In about ½ mile you come to a fork. Fork right to a nearby T-junction and turn left, still on a wooded track. Look out for a finger post and ****Note** the path up to the right for the return walk.

Continue towards the coast on your wide woodland track. It bends to the right to a junction. The track ahead is 'Private'. You have to turn left. In ¼ mile you pass a stone cottage down on the left, once the home of those who worked the lime kiln that was on the beach. Mouthmill Cove is below.

You have views over the sea to Lundy Island and rocky cliffs nearby.

Turn right and follow the Coast Path uphill under trees. *You are climbing above the track that brought you here.* Avoid a path to the left unless you want a longish diversion to 'Lookout'. Instead, keep climbing to Gallantry Bower. *Markers on the way indicate the grid reference points.*

Mouthmill Cove

After a climb of ¼ mile, you emerge to open downland with views on all sides. *Down to the right, see the track through fields of the return walk.*

Re-enter woods on the Coast Path. You soon come to rest on seats in *a wooden shelter carved by Sir James Hamlyn Williams in 1826, known as 'Angels Wings'.* Heave yourself off the seat and keep going gently downhill through woodland for ¼ mile.

Turn right into a track signposted 'to the Church'. This is a permissive path in the Clovelly Estate. Carry on down through larch trees. In ½ mile turn left along the estate road to Clovelly Church.

To visit the village of Clovelly, continue on the Church access lane past the walled garden to the village road. Turn left to pass the Visitor Centre on the right. *You may be in time to catch a bus here to Hartland or Bideford.*

Visitors to Clovelly pay an entrance fee towards the upkeep of the village.

To return to Brownsham on the Coast Path, *walk down through the cobbled streets to the Harbour and turn left on a road past the pub and up Brownsham Cliff to retrace your steps to Mouthmill. (Really seasoned walkers may want to carry on the Coast Path as far as Hartland Point and beyond but this is a very tough walk of over 12 miles with precipitous cliffs).*

To return to Brownsham on the inland path, from Clovelly Church retrace your steps past the Estate Offices and along the lane past the familiar permissive path on the right. Keep going through farm cottages on the track that leads to 'Snacksland'. In ¼ mile you are directed off this track into the field on the right. *Enjoy crossing the open field towards woodland and look up to your earlier cliff walk.*

Avoid the field corner and make for a gate beside the wood. Walk down to another gate to enter Brownsham Wood. Cross to the rough stony track opposite. This leads you back to the familiar woodland track, noted above.**

Turn left then right to climb back up to Brownsham Car Park.

Walk 11: Abbotsham, South West Coast Path to Alwington

A combination of wild coast path and country lanes link churches today that were neighbours before busy roads got in the way.

Starting Point: Green Cliff, west of Abbotsham. Parking on the Farm £1
GR411268 Map: OS Explorer 126 **Terrain:** rugged remote Coast Path and country lanes **Distance:** 10 Miles (3½ Miles South West Coast Path)
Local Information: Lime Kiln at Greencliff once produced lime fertiliser.
Portledge Manor House was the home of local landowners, named Coffin. William the Conqueror gave Alwington to the Coffin family. Parts of the house date from 1234. It is mainly a handsome 17th century manor house. The Coffins were obliged to sell their estates in late 20th century due to tax problems. Their last property was sold in 1998. Portledge House became a hotel. It is now private. The public has no access.
Fortunately the **National Trust** bought and manages the Coast Path also Peppercombe Valley.
**'Gifford`s Jump'** may be based on a real event but details are scarce. A careless young man on a seaside picnic in 1537, leant back and fell over the cliff`s edge, 120 feet? He survived unscathed. You might not be so lucky!
Buses: Stagecoach 319 calls in at Fairy Cross at 10.55. 13.16, 15.21 and 18.56 on its way from Hartland to Bideford and will drop you at Abbotsham. To check times phone Traveline 0871 200 2233 It may not run on Sundays.
Warning: Once you are on the Coast Path there is no escape for 3 miles. Only seasoned walkers should attempt this walk and should choose clement weather

The Churches

Abbotsham, St Helen. A chapel on a cliff overlooking the sea stood about 1 mile away from today`s village in around the year 1100. It was in the care of Tavistock Abbey. As the population of Abbotsham increased, a new church was built inland in 13th century. The chapel became a ruin and is now lost, apart from the round Norman fluted font that was transferred to the new church where it has a place of honour. St Helen`s still has some windows from the 13th century; the lancet windows in nave and chancel are original. Other window frames are 16th century. In 1300 or thereabouts, the tower was built on the south side. Two small windows above the chancel arch were there to light up the rood loft. By 1561 it was illegal for all churches to have rood lofts so that in Abbotsham is sealed. The rood screen was also dismantled. The church has retained medieval ceilings over nave, chancel and south transept. The chancel has bosses. The nave has angels with shields. In 18th century the church was able to fund several almshouses and provide lessons in

Abbotsham to Alwington

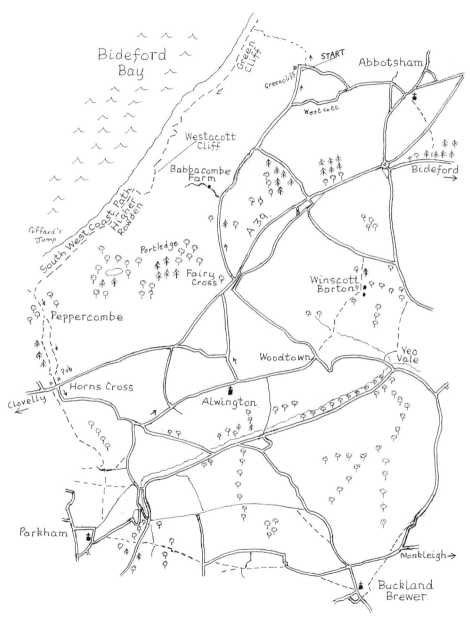

Abbotsham

reading to 8 poor children. But by 19th century restoration of the fabric was needed. Mrs E. Vidal describes the state of the church: dirty, damp and smelling from the vaults. The roof ribs were painted bright blue and the angels brilliant yellow. The Victorians rectified these deficiencies and also added stained glass to some windows. The bench ends in the south transept are Victorian. Other panels date from 1520 and some may have come from monasteries dissolved in 1540. There are 39 bench ends in all. The pulpit was installed in 1896.

Alwington, St Andrew presents immediate charm in its quiet setting and lovely view over to Buckland. *The church is locked. To gain entrance we had to phone the number written in the porch (not the Rector of 1278!) It has a lovely interior.*

The next thought is 'where have all the people gone? For this is quite a big church with a tall tower in three stages and grand pinnacles. The two projecting gargoyles are called 'bulldogs' locally. The only habitations are scattered houses and farms. Outside the tower are the remains of a 13th century preaching cross. On the south door is a sanctuary handle for fugitives to grasp and claim asylum. The church itself is originally 13th century with modifications over the years. It consists of chancel, nave, north transept, and south aisle with 5 bays and granite monoliths from Lundy Island. In 1789 the wagon roofs were given new ceilings. New windows were inserted in the north wall. The church contains some fascinating oddments. The font has a Saxon base, a Norman shaft and a 13th century basin with inscribed symbols. Barum tiles are set in the nave floor. The pulpit is made up with old bench ends. The reredos is made of bits of the rood screen from Parkham Church. In the

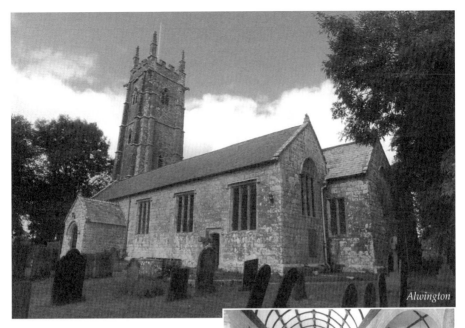

Alwington

south aisle is a stage, once the minstrels` gallery from Portledge Tudor Manor House. Windows in the east end of the south aisle contains some very old stained glass at the top. Other windows contain Victorian glass. There is a memorial to the Pine-Coffin family from Portledge House (see above). This lovely church houses the famous 'Alwington Bible', a series of carvings by Reuben Arnold. They are 21 bench ends that tell the story of the Old and New Testaments. He completed them in 1925.

The Walk

You may choose to visit Abbotsham Church then drive to Greencliff along the narrow lane opposite. A sign advertises parking here.

From the Farm Car Park, which is also a camp site, walk back along the access lane and in 25 metres turn left into an enclosed footpath. The path heads north then turns left towards the sea where Lundy Island seems quite near. In ½ mile you reach the South West Coast Path at Green Cliff. Below you see a line of large grey pebbles on the beach. Turn left.

The National Trust notice warns that care must be taken on the Coast Path since there has been erosion. We are fortunate that their team has been at work improving drainage and steps, putting in boardwalks and stones in places and pruning hedges.

The geology here has made some of this coast a Site of Scientific Interest.

The cliffs ahead are not particularly high. You pass over farmland and climb the sweeping slopes of Cockington Cliff. A ladder stile is in good repair. Hartland Point can be seen on a clear day. Gorse bushes are on Higher Rowden. You may catch glimpses of Portledge Manor House but the grounds are private. Giffard's Jump is somewhere near here (see Local Information above). The Coast Path comes down to sea level then rises towards the craggy heights of Peppercombe Castle. You are spared this steeper climb for you reach a wooded valley first. After 3 miles of coastal walk, turn left at Peppercombe Valley.

You now have a steady climb through woodland. It seems a very long mile before you reach the A39 at Horns Cross and a welcome pub.

Cross the main road to the lane opposite and walk past a small residential area. The road bends left then in ½ mile you reach crossroads. Cross diagonally right and keep on course to a nearby fork in the road. Fork left and continue up the lane for nearly 1 mile to Alwington Church. You go throught the car park on the right to find the secluded church.

From Alwington Church, return through the car park to the lane and turn right to nearby Town Farm at crossroads. Turn left and follow another lane to Fairy Cross, a hamlet that straddles the A39.

If you wish to take the bus to Abbotsham, cross the A39 to the bus stop.

To continue walking the lanes, turn right just before the main road, A39 then at a point further along the main road, cross to the lane opposite. This leads for 2 miles past Babbacombe Farm and Cockington Farm. At Westacott you can turn right to Abbotsham but may prefer to keep left, heading north to pick up your vehicle at Greencliff.

Green Cliff

5 Walks near Honiton

Walk 12: Axminster to Hawkchurch

From a spacious minster church follow the river then lanes and fields over hill and vale to a village church rich in Norman and Early English carvings

Starting Point: Axminster Parish Church   **GR**296986
See Map opposite for Railway Station or possible Parking on North Street
Map: OS Explorer 116 **Terrain:** Undulating countryside   **Distance:** 8 Miles
Local Information: 1. Cistercian Newenham Abbey was founded by the Mohuns in 1245. Lower Abbey Farm, southwest of Axminster is on the site?
2. Axminster carpets were established 1755 by local weaver Thomas Whitty.
3. Wyld Court, Hawkchurch is the old manor house, converted into cottages.
4. The Old Inn existed for builders of the Church, Hawkchurch, according to the landlady. This may be true but the present Inn has a stone dated 1547.
Note: The footpaths were just passable after the wettest March on record.
On the map, I have indicated a possible alternative past Cuthays and along Evil Lane. Chaos ruled at Cuthays and Evil Lane lived up to its name.

The Churches
The Parish Church of St Mary the Virgin, Axminster. In 899 King Alfred mentioned the Royal Manor of Axanmynster; 'Axan' means water. The Saxon church has vanished but there is an Anglo-Saxon or Norman doorway with colonettes and chevrons. It has been re-sited and can be seen from the outside, in the east wall of

Axeminster

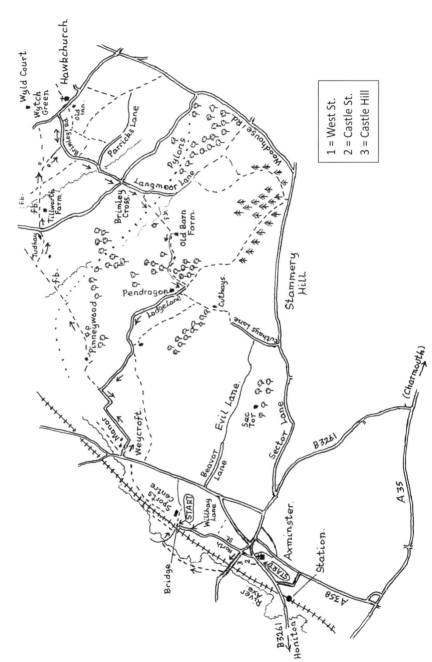

Axminster to Hawkchurch

1 = West St.
2 = Castle St.
3 = Castle Hill

the south chapel. The present church dates from the 13th century with a sturdy tower at the crossing. The tower was damaged in the Civil War when Puritans from Lyme came to attack Royalists in Axminster. Plaster was used to repair it until in 1898 it was encased in Beer stone. The Church has undergone many changes. For example the transepts have been absorbed in the north and south aisles. In 15th century a chantry was added to the chancel on north side and in 16th century the north aisle was extended the length of the nave. The parapet above this aisle displays badges, the Stafford knot and Courtenay roundels, also shields and gargoyles. The two-storey north porch was added 1525–30, the upper part originally a priest`s room. Inside, the piers at the crossing are 13th century, as are the chancel west walls. Two effigies are in the chancel. On the south side lies Alicia de Mohun who died around 1257. In the north wall lies Gervase de Prestaller. The small Gothic side windows of the chancel are probably 14th century. Most other windows in the church are 19th or 20th century. The chancel aisle of 1480 is a chapel, the rest of the south aisle was added in 1800. The Nave is spacious with four bays between nave and aisles on both sides. Victorian restoration vandalised the capitals. However some improvement came from raising the ceiling in 1834 to make room for clerestory windows. Today the Church is a meeting place where there are many activities including concerts. What a blessed situation the church has on the Green in the centre of town!

St John the Baptist, Hawkhurst stands prominently in an elevated village. 'Havoc`s Church' or 'Avekchurch' stands above small fields, woods and farms that survive from Saxon times. The present church has outstanding Norman and Early English carvings. The chancel arch has Norman carvings of dragons on the north capital and scallops on the south capital. The pointed chancel arch is Medieval. The north arcade in Norman style has low piers and wide arches, similar to Farway and

Hawkhurst

Membury. The Early English south arcade balances that of the north. The arches are a little higher and the fine carvings may have come from the workshop of Wells Cathedral. Victorian alterations include a clerestory in late Norman style. Carvings of faces from the corbel table were set high outside on both sides of the nave. They are beautiful Norman carvings that deserve more attention.

Norman carvings, St John the Baptist. Photo: Peter Park

The Walk

With your back to Axminster Church cross West Street to the shops opposite and turn right. In 75 metres turn left into Castle Street. Continue down Castle Hill to a level crossing over the railway, then a stone bridge over the River Axe. Here are cottages in a rural setting.

After the bridge, turn right into a footpath between cottages. Head north over meadows. There is a wooded hill ahead. The river is away to your right. After a short enclosed section, the footpath joins the river hurrying through flat meadows below the wooded hill, Cloakham.

Too soon you come to a private bridge carrying the driveway up to Cloakham. Join the driveway and turn right to cross the bridge over the river. Walk along the driveway away from the hill and the river. Just before a private railway bridge*, turn left to descend into more meadows.

If you have parked in North Street, continue on foot to the fork in the road and veer left into Willhay Lane. This winds to the private railway bridge above. Turn right to descend into the meadows.*

You now have the railway line on your right for half a mile when signposts point the way to the rail crossing.

Cross the rail track with care and you come to a tarmac path. Turn left and walk on this smooth tarmac for ¼ mile to A358. Cross this road diagonally left towards the Manor and Weycroft House. Avoid the footpath in the left corner. Instead walk up the no-through-road, Lodge Lane. This passes the houses and bends to the left to lead northeast on an elevated course.

In ½ mile at another bend with signposts, you leave the lane and keep straight on along a track to Pinneywood. The track curves to the right and descends to a lone cottage.

Pass the cottage on the left and look up to two small copses on the right. Cross the field uphill to the second copse. Pass this copse on the right then turn left. Follow the hedge on the right for ¼ mile to a field corner.

Go through a gap in the hedge to join a track serving pylons. **STOP!** High on this track, you have views over the Axe Valley and its tributary below. There is no clear footpath sign. Look down into the valley below to discern a footbridge over a stream. Clamber down over tussocks continuing northwest in the field. Cross the footbridge.

On the other side follow the hedge on the left as you climb in another field up towards a tree line. Over to the right you will see another lone cottage. When you are level with this cottage, keep on course for another 50 metres then turn right. Head towards the cottage, crossing a footbridge into the next field. Turn left and follow the hedge on the left. You come up to further cottages in Cadhay. Veer left to walk along their access lane.

The access lane leads to a byway. Cross diagonally right to the driveway to Tillworth Farm. Pass a seat and keep going towards the farmhouse. Just before the farmhouse, cross a stile in the hedge on the left. From the height of this stile look down to Fairwater, the stream below. Avoid a high footbridge down to the left. Instead, keep on course towards Hawkchurch, seen ahead. Pass over a mound to find a smaller footbridge below. The water was fair with snowdrops in March.

On the other side a lovely sloping field has trees in its hedges. At a stile in the hedge opposite you have a choice of ways. I have chosen to go straight on towards thatched cottages on the edge of Hawkchurch. Turn right on their access lane and climb for ¼ mile up to Brimley Road.

Turn left and continue climbing past cottages to crossroads at Wytch Green. *Wyld Court is to the left.* The Church and Old Inn are to the right.

From Hawkchurch return down Brimley Road, passing the familiar access lane on right. Continue downhill heading southwest to the hamlet of Brimley where you fork right, avoiding Parrick`s Lane. In about 1 mile from Hawkchurch you come to Brimley Cross. Cross to Langmoor Lane opposite and keep on course for under ¼ mile. At crosspaths turn right. In March we had to climb a bank on the left to pass through the muddy field entrance.

The field ahead is sprinkled with patches of sedge. Nonetheless we managed to squelch down to the footbridge over a stream in the strip of woodland below. As you descend, keep in sight of a lone house on the other side of the hedge on the left.

Once you have crossed to the next field, you have a gentle climb up towards Old Barn Farm. Keep just to the right of this farmhouse to join its access track and turn right. The access track takes a winding course up through woodland. The relief of finding a firm track under foot mitigates sorrow at the sight of rusting farm equipment, abandoned in the woodland.

You come up to Lodge Lane at Pendragon with a war shelter on the left and a detached house on the right. *You may see footpaths opposite but mud and misfortune have deterred me from recommending them, see Note above.*

Turn right along Lodge Lane and follow its twists and turns for over one mile past the familiar track to Pinneywood and the Manor House at Weycroft. Re-cross A358 and join the smooth tarmac track again.

Either retrace your steps over the railway to Axminster.

Or keep on the smooth track to Sports Centre at the outskirts of that town.

Walk 13: Shute Barton to Loughwood Meeting House

An ancient route from Axminster to Colyton was also taken by Baptists to their Chapel, hidden in the woods. Visit two National Trust properties.

Starting Point: the entrance to Shute Barton National Trust property **GR**253974
Map: OS Explorer 116
Terrain: Tracks and footpaths, quite Hilly   **Distance:** 8 Miles
Local Information: Shute Barton is a medieval manor house, now National Trust holiday homes. For details of opening Phone 01752 346585
Warning: 1. On the return walk, * 'travellers' with their caravans are on the Roman road west of Kilmington. I have been unable to find an alternative route apart from retracing your steps over the fields.
2. ** Before taking the footpath route, read on to 'Obstacles'. You might prefer Haddon Road!

The Churches

The Church of St Michael, Shute was a 13th century chapel of Colyton Church. It stands on an ancient route from Axminster to Colyton. It was an Early English church with a central tower, chancel, nave and transepts. The tower has stayed

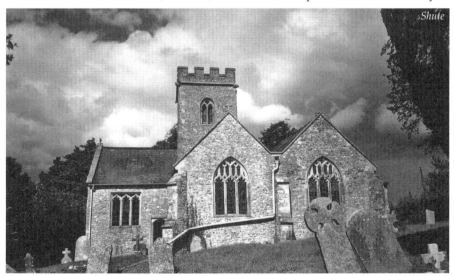

Shute

intact. The rest was enlarged when the Lady Chapel was added in 15th century. The east window of this chapel has some fine heraldic glass. Beer stone has been used for window and door frames. Chert from Shute Hill is the main fabric of the church. In 19th century the north aisle was added. There is much Victorian restoration, some

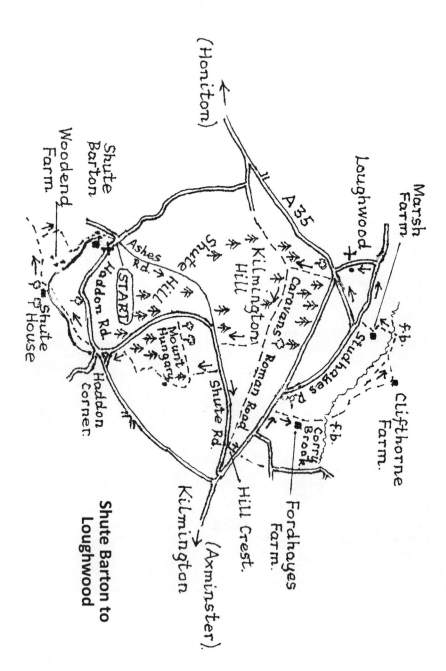

**Shute Barton to
Loughwood**

very beautiful such as the roof bosses of the chancel and wrought iron grille between chancel and north aisle. A panel framed in alabaster depicts Margaret Pole meeting her three little daughters at the gate of heaven – 'her equally aspirant infants' as Pevsner cynically says. The 15th century font has a cover with wrought iron.

Loughwood Meeting House is a 17th century cottage, once sequestered in woodland and converted into a chapel by Baptists who had to hide from

Loughwood

persecution. They came from local towns and villages to be baptised in the pool under boards near the table and pulpit. Members from Shute and Colyton would make for the boundary stone on the old Roman road of our walk. Probably they founded the footpath down to the main road to cross to the lane down to Loughwood. The National Trust has restored this chapel to its original rustic beauty with thatched roof, 19th century box pews and west gallery. Players of stringed instruments were in the gallery.

The Walk

Outside the entrance to Shute Barton, cross the Green to the telephone booth and seat. Turn up the nearby lane, 'unsuitable for traffic'. This is Ashes Road. It becomes a stony track up Shute Hill. Keep to the track as it swings to the left and emerges from woodland. In 1 kilometre avoid the path to the right and continue through more woodland on Kilmington Hill.

Join Shute Road and keep on course. Note the footpath on the left for the return walk. Go down Shute Road past occasional houses to Kilmington in ½ mile. Avoid the track on the left. Take the short residential road 'Hill Crest' down to the A35.

Turn left and walk along the pavement for ¼ mile. Cross with care to the path opposite leading down to Fordhayes Farm. Head north over the open meadow and down to fast flowing Corry Brook, a tributary of the Yarty.

Cross the strong new footbridge over the brook. Turn left to follow the brook for a short distance. Head up towards but not too close to the Farm on the hillside. Keep to the lower slopes heading westwards over the fields until you come to a path on the left and another footbridge over the brook. Damp enclosed terrain here contrasts with the open ground of the first footbridge about ½ mile away.

Find your way through mud to nearby Marsh Farm. Go through the farmyard and turn right to Studhayes Road. Here you have a choice:

Hilly Route: Cross diagonally left to a farm track up to the main road. Turn immediately right and walk down the steep lane to Loughwood Chapel.

Road Route: Turn right and walk along Studhayes Road for ¼ mile to crossroads. Turn left for Loughwood Chapel.

From Loughwood Meeting House walk uphill along the lane to A35. Cross with care to the footpath opposite. The path under trees is muddy at first as you keep to a boundary on the left. Climb through woodland heading south up to a T-junction. Turn left and walk along the Roman road. *Travellers (see note above) have set up camp here. Walk past their caravans heading southeast for nearly ½ mile.

Turn right into a steep rocky footpath up Kilmington Hill. In ¼ mile you reach familiar Shute Road. *For the shortest way back to Shute*, *turn right and retrace your steps over Shute Hill and down Ashes Road.*

For the longer alternative route, turn left. Walk for 100 metres along Shute Road. Turn right into a bridleway. At T-junction turn left and then right. Go down to another junction and turn right into a dry path through fir trees. Pass a lone house on the left. In ¼ mile the path bends to the right and leads to the entrance to Mount Hungary Nature Reserve. We have made a tour of the edge of this nature reserve.

Go to the nearby road and turn left to the green junction, Haddon Corner. Turn sharp right into **Haddon Road**. It leads back to Shute Church (1 km).

For footpaths, a path on the left joins the drive down to Shute House. Walk past the front of the house and **Stop! There is a hidden enclosed path beside the wooded grounds on the left. You come to a field and cross to search for stile in the hedge opposite. On the other side of the hedge, chaos rules. Woodend Farm is over to the right. Your aim is to pass it on your right. First, find a way over a stream hidden in tussocks to an electric fence across the footpath. Go through a gateway deep in slurry to find the path to Shute Barton on the right. Turn left and follow the walls on your right.

Walk 14: Colyton to Seaton and Beer

Descend on the tramway through the Axe Valley to the Sea at Seaton. Walk on the coastal path to the picturesque seaside village of Beer and return on foot through nature reserves. Three churches are open to visitors.

Starting Point: Car Park for the Tramway at Colyton, off Station Road.
No parking charge for tram users. Café, shop, ticket office and Tram Stop are on other side of the line. Ticket approx. £6 single journey   **GR**252940
Map: OS Explorer 116   **Distance:** 9 miles walk can be shorter, 3 miles tram
Terrain: Flat promenade by the sea, possible cliff climbs (see Note below), gentle hills inland, some lanes. Consult the map to check on their names.
Information: Trams run everyday from 10 a.m. in season (April – 5 Nov)
         Some weekends only in February and March.
         Also opens 27th Dec. to 7th Jan.   Phone 01297 20375
Beer (Bearu in Old English) was a quiet fishing village hidden by cliffs.
 It has become a tourist attraction best avoided by car.
 Note: A cliff fall between Seaton and Beer has led to the closure of the Coast Path, as shown below*, and a diversion onto the pavement of B3172.

Churches
The Parish Church of St Andrew, Colyton presides over this Saxon town. Ancient

Colyton

Colyton to Seaton via the Tramway

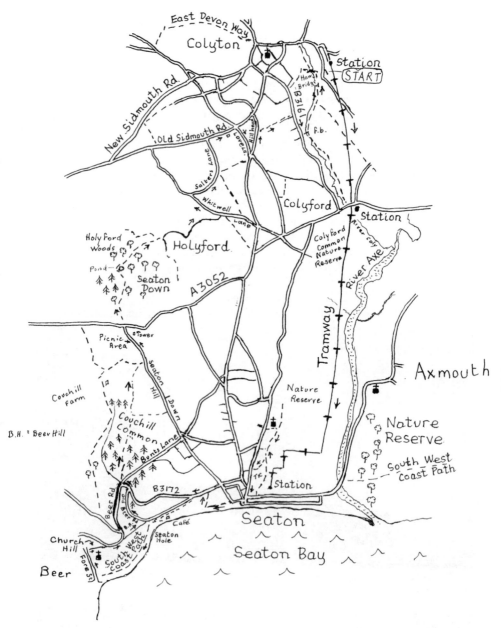

stone and flint buildings cluster around it. Little lanes lead to and fro. A Saxon church was here from 700 AD, it was the mother church of the district. In 1933 after a fire, carved stones were found in the west face of the tower. They have been assembled and placed in the south transept to form the finest Saxon cross in Devon. In 12th century a cruciform Norman church with central tower replaced the Saxon one. The chancel and transepts are the same shape that they were in Norman times. The central tower with Norman base still dominates. Colyton was one of the great wool towns in the Middle Ages. Wool merchants contributed to church building. In 14th and 15th centuries the nave was made taller and a huge west window was added. It was later filled with glass provided by modern donors. The east

Colyton

window is early 14th century. The distinctive lantern tower was built above the parapets so that it overlooks Colyton. Wool merchants may have brought the idea of a lantern from Bruges. There are only two like it in England. In 1769 the south aisle was enlarged and has round arches. The north aisle was built 50 years later. The aisles are wide and make for space in the nave. The oldest monument of around 1450 is to Margaret Beauford. It was moved from the north transept to the chancel. On either side of the chancel are chapels. The Yonge family from the Great House,

Seaton

Colyton had a private chapel, now The Lady Chapel on the north side. It has a stone Jacobean screen The Pole family chapel is on the south side. The stone screen here is 16th century. The Pole family from Shute still own much of the land hereabouts.

St Gregory, Seaton stood above Axmouth Harbour when ships, carrying wool and bringing back spirits, sailed past in 14th century. Windows of that period have survived in the south chapel and north aisle. The church has a low 15th century west tower. The rest has changed considerably over the years. The church has retained its 19th century gallery at the west end. A window, 'The Waters of Life' was engraved by Simon Whistler in 2001.

Beer

The Parish Church of Beer, St Michael the Archangel was completely rebuilt in Decorated style in 1870. Beer stone from the local quarry and blue limestone were used. There may have been a church here in 12th century when Beer and Seaton both came under Sherborne Abbey and had to supply wine, fish, salt and fodder to the monks. 1650 the Walronds of Bovey House to the northwest held the Manor and may have built the church. A daughter married Lord Rolle who sponsored the present building. He has a memorial near the tower. The church is on a steep slope so the chancel is higher than the nave. Stained glass from the old church is in a roundel near the font.

The Walk

Catch the tram from Colyton and enjoy the run down through Axe estuary.

At the Seaton tramway terminus, pass the nearby Tourist Information Centre and continue northwards across the large Car Park towards Underfleet. In the far left hand corner of the Car Park head towards a Play Area and you join the Cycle Route, Wessex Way. Keep on course and in under ½ mile you reach Seaton Church.

For those who want a shorter walk, The Wessex Way leads northwards through Nature Reserves towards Colyford.

From Seaton Church to Beer, retrace your steps along Wessex Way as far as the Car Park. Turn right away from the Car Park and cross B3172, 'the Underfleet' to climb up to Marsh Road. This leads to Fore Street. Turn left and walk down past shops and cafes to the sea at Marine Place.

Cross with care to the Esplanade and turn right. This is a delightful walk along

Seaton

the seafront towards the cliffs that screen Beer. Too soon you come to the end of the promenade at the Chine and have to climb up steps on the right, past toilets and gardens to West Cliffe Terrace, sea view apartments.

The main Beer Road B3714 is ahead. Cross to the pavement on the other side and walk uphill past detached houses. **Note: The first road on the left, Old Beer Road was and should be the route of the South Devonshire Coast Path. Unfortunately at the time of writing, due to cliff falls, it is closed. If or when it opens, you can continue on this well defined cliff walk to Beer.*

If the Coast Path is still closed, continue uphill on the pavement along B3714. In ½ mile you come to the other part of Old Beer Road on the left. ***The way back to Colyton*** *is 50 metres further along B3714. If you wish to shorten the walk, omitting Beer, turn right here into* <u>*Bunts Lane*</u> *(See below)*

To continue to Beer, turn left into Old Beer Road and head down beside Beer Brook to Seaton Hole where sea views, refreshments and toilets are available. Climb out of Seaton Hole the way you came and turn left to join the undulating Coast Path to Beer, a distance of over ½ mile. As you approach, you pass seats on the cliff side for sea views. At Beer you come down to the bottom of Fore Street. Turn right onto the lower end of this street. Walk up Fore Street away from the sea to Beer Church on the right.

From Beer Church turn sharp right and climb steeply up the narrow lane, Church Hill. It brings you back to B3174.

Turn right to find a path through edge of a field. Next you come to the road, Beer Hill leading down towards Seaton Hole. On the other side of Beer Brooke, just before the bottom, turn left up Old Beer Hill.

At the top cross diagonally left to <u>Bunts Lane</u>. Go down 75 metres to crossways in the valley of Beer Brook. Avoid Couchill Farm Lane on the left and cross to the footpath opposite. The firm path is well established uphill where conifers have been cleared from Couchill Common. You join a track heading due north on a ledge above the valley on the left. At a fork in the way and in the absence of signs to the contrary, I took the track following the telegraph poles. It overlooks the valley and Couchill Farm. *In ½ mile a path joins from the right.*

Do not turn right but keep on course through elevated woodland for another ½ mile to emerge at Seaton Down Hill. *Pause to enjoy the views over Seaton to the River Axe and to the left, farmland.*

Continue north over downland towards the white building of a grand water tower. Avoid the path to the left to Gatcombe Farm and head towards the road, B3172. Turn left to walk beside the road up to a nearby picnic area.

You are now at the top of the hill and keep on course to pass the Water Tower and a petrol station on the right. Ahead is the A3052.

Cross this busy road with care to the haven of a footpath, opposite left. A new view opens over countryside to the north. Walk downhill through a steeply sloping field, with the hedge on your right. You enter Holyford Woods at an information post. *This is the country`s thousandth nature reserve where oak, ash and hazel prevail and dormice find a home.*

Follow the path, downhill still. The first slope has been cleared of fir trees. Avoid permissive cross tracks. Go down to the dank bottom where there is a dark pond. Cross a footbridge to circumnavigate the pond. Keep on the path through the wood northeastwards. *Holyford Brook is unseen on the right.*

Leave Holyford Woods to find a delightful meadow where you keep on course. Avoid the path to the left and make for the houses of Holyford Hamlet. *You now have to walk on lanes as footpaths were very muddy.*

Walk along the access road, the winding Holyford Lane for ½ mile to Whitwell Lane. Turn left and walk for under ¼ mile to turn right into nearby Salters Lane. This narrow lane climbs northwards to Old Sidmouth Road at the top. Turn right and walk on the verge passing a detached house on the right. At crossroads turn right and walk along Love Lane to more crossroads. Turn left into Hillhead. Here the houses on your right have a good view over the River Axe.

You come to a picnic site and turn right into a short footpath that heads northeast down the field slope to Newbery Close. Go through the few houses to the main Coly Road, B3161. Cross to the playing field opposite and turn right to walk beside the road for 200 metres to a footpath on the left.

Here is a footbridge over the River Coly. On the other side turn left to walk beside the river for ¼ mile. Then veer gradually right across meadows towards Colyford Tram Station. At Cownhayne Lane turn left then sharp right to the Car Park.

Walk 15: Gittisham to Ottery St Mary

Take a quiet walk across fields and lanes from a village to a town with the most magnificent church. Both places have escaped the fast lane and retain their Devonshire character

Starting Point: Gittisham Church   **GR**134984   **Map:** OS Explorer 115
Narrow lanes lead to Gittisham. You may prefer to start in Ottery
Terrain: Undulating, traffic free, almost linear   **Distance:** 8-9 Miles
This can be halved if you decide to take a bus
Local Information:
Gittisham is an ancient village with some cob and thatch cottages.
Combe House, now a hotel on the slopes of Gittisham Hill is Elizabethan.
Bronze Age Barrows on Gittisham Hill stretch for 3 miles southeastwards
Bus 380 plies between Ottery and Gittisham, Monday to Saturday at about two hourly intervals   Phone traveline 0871 200 2233

The Churches
Gittisham, St Michael is unprepossessing on the outside, as it is flint, covered in cement. Only the Perpendicular south aisle has escaped this covering. External steps by the tower lead up to the gallery. Inside, it is barn-like with high wagon roofs. Civil War damage was repaired by William Putt in 1662. The box pews of 1715 and the gallery, even earlier, give an air of the 18th century. In fact the church is first

Gittisham

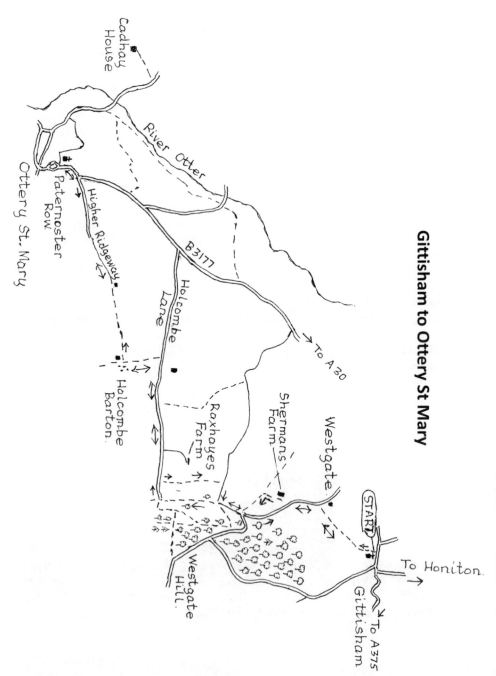

Gittisham to Ottery St Mary

mentioned in 1279 and is still mainly Early English. The chancel was restored in 19th century, including the 14th century chancel arch. The east window of 1873 has good glass depicting the Ascension. There are several monuments in the south aisle.

St Mary of Ottery. A church existed here from 12th century. Edward the Confessor

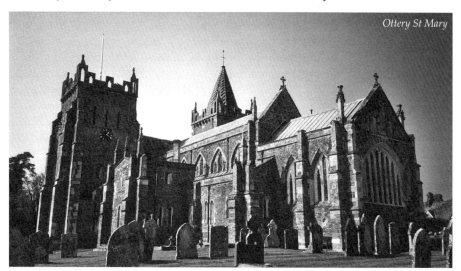

Ottery St Mary

gave the manor of Ottery to the Canons of Rouen Cathedral, in 1061 and so they came into possession of the church. In 1280 the church was leased to Walter de Lechelade, Precentor of Exeter. As agent for Rouen, he exacted rent and also took pickings for himself. He was murdered in the cathedral yard. The Church avenged his death on the lay people who were hanged. The clergy, including Wolfrington, Vicar of Ottery had prison sentences. In 1328, Bishop of Exeter, John de Grandisson chose Ottery St Mary as an ideal site for conversion to a collegiate church. It took him until 1333 to settle terms with the 'unreasonable and exorbitant' canons. In 1337 Edward 111 granted a licence for the collegiate church. The college had 40 members. The new building was modelled on Exeter Cathedral and completed in 1342 all of a piece. It is the grandest church in Devon. As at Exeter there are two transeptal towers and, inside, the uninterrupted view extends from west to east. The nave has five bays with early Perpendicular arches. The chancel with north and south aisles is in Early English style. It is longer than the nave. The roof bosses in the crossing vault are superb. The windows have many lights in a single arch. The Dorset aisle with fine fan vaulted roof was added in 16th century. The carving is exceptional throughout this church.

For more details see the Short History and Guide by John A. Whitham.

The Walk

Face Gittisham Church and take the footpath on the right. It starts on a lane past the church then some cottages at the back. It dwindles to a track and becomes a well marked path across fields.

Follow the hedge on the right. You have a view to the hill over to the left, known locally as Tommy Wax Hill. In ¼ mile cross a footbridge over a stream. In the next field climb diagonally left up to a farm gate. *Most walkers have gone round the left hand edge of the field.* Again, follow the hedge on the right, passing the gate into a cottage garden. Then turn sharp right to climb a stile into a lane. *The cottage is on your right.*

Turn left and walk along the lane to nearby Shermans Farm. **For the field route** *enter the farmyard to find a gate on the left and head up through cows to a crosstrack. Turn left onto this bridleway and walk to a junction.*

For the road route, continue up the lane for ¼ mile passing woodland on the left. You approach a bend. Turn right at a bridleway sign on the right.

Both routes: Ignore the bridleway and follow a track heading south through the woods. This track is not favoured with a signpost. It soon leads to crossways. Avoid both the 'unmetalled road' on the right and the bridleway on the left. Instead, cross to the footpath opposite and continue south through the woods. You are on the edge of Westgate Hill. In ½ mile of woodland you pass a shed and a lone cottage. You emerge to the top end of Holcombe Lane and enjoy a view over rolling fields, mainly pastureland.

Turn right and walk down Holcombe Lane for nearly a mile. On the way **note** the first footpath on the right for the return walk. Pass the entrance to Raxhayes Farm then the second footpath on the right opposite Higher Holcombe. When you reach a nursery on the right you are nearly at your turning.

Turn left to Holcombe Barton. Here is a pleasant track shaded by trees. In ¼ mile you reach farm buildings on the right. **Stop just before the farm!** Turn right into a hedged path leading to fields. Keep on course uphill. You are heading towards a fine modern conversion of a cottage. Pass this on you right and you are on its long straight access road.

Higher Ridgeway leads through the outskirts of Ottery St Mary. After 1 mile of this long straight road, you come to the B3177. Turn left for the church and town centre.

From Ottery St Mary, if you wish to avoid retracing you steps, take the bus back to Gittisham (see local information above).

To return on foot to Gittisham, retrace your steps along Higher Ridgeway, past Holcombe Barton and up Holcombe Lane as far as the noted footpath. Turn left here and follow the hedge on the left. Roxhayes Farm is below on your left and the woodland of Westgate Hill on your right. In ½ mile you come to the unmetalled road. Turn right and walk up to the familiar crossways. Turn left into the woodland path, not favoured with a signpost and retrace your steps to Gittisham.

Walk 16: Awliscombe to Buckerell

Medieval village churches on either side of a hill are joined by a footpath

Starting Point: The village car park, shared with the pub above A373 main road, Awliscombe **GR**133018 **Map:** OS Explorer 115 **Terrain:** Hilly
Distance: 4 Miles **Note:** The alternative route back is confined and muddy.
You may prefer to retrace your steps over the hill.

The Churches
The Church of St Mary and St Giles, Buckerell is described as 'a charming example of vernacular architecture' and the interior indeed has this character. The outside stonework is covered and the rendering detracts from its charm. The first definite

Buckerell

record of a church here occurs in 1258 when Bishop of Exeter, Walter Bronscombe appointed two chaplains to 'Bockerel' and began registers, the oldest in the diocese. It was a cruciform building with a low tower. In 1287 Bishop Quivil noted that parishioners were quarrelling over seats. 1319 is the accepted date when the church was dedicated. Then in 1330 commissioners of the Dean and Chapter of Exeter found the church to be 'ruinous' but praised the vicar for his care of his flock. Bishop Stafford (1395-1419) had many churches repaired and it is believed that Buckerell

Awliscombe to Buckerell

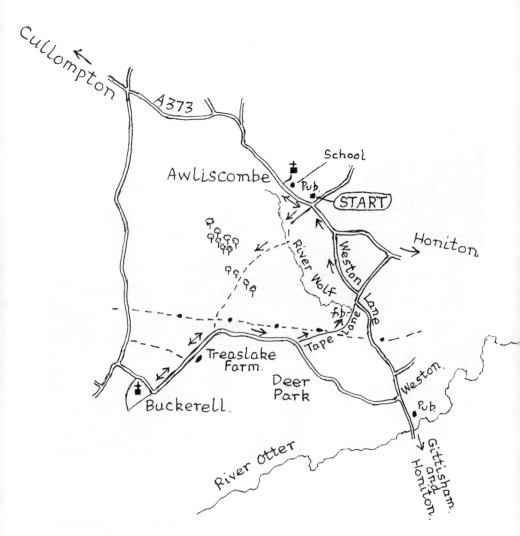

was one of them. A stone is inscribed with the date 1403. Most windows and door frames are of an earlier style but those in the transepts are Perpendicular and probably part of Bishop Stafford`s work. The nave has a wagon roof with bosses. The west tower in three stages was built, replacing a bell turret. There are now six bells. The rood screen from another setting was introduced and fitted between chancel and nave. Arguments over seating persisted so that Bishops had seating plans made. One plan of 1773 has survived and shows the separation of men and women. 'Poor men' were in the north transept and 'poor women' at the west end. Husbands and wives were apart and the men at the front! Today eighteenth century pews fill the nave and transepts. The gallery holds an organ of 1907.

St Michael and All Angels, Awliscombe stands on an elevated pagan site with a standing stone outside the west door. Today the A373 passes below. There are some

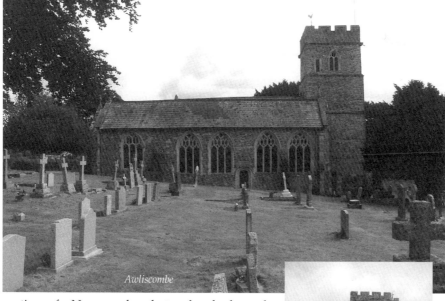

Awliscombe

Awliscombe

vestiges of a Norman church: two heads above the window near the porch, a corbel table in the south wall of the nave and an arch above the south door. In 12th century the church was in the diocese of Exeter. Bishop William Brewer gave it to Dunkeswell Abbey where it remained until the Dissolution. The nave was rebuilt at the end of 13th century and slopes up to the east end. The church has an early 16th century chancel screen of Beer stone, described by Arthur Mee: 'its leafy arch resting on rich capitals and its six angels projecting from the mullions'. There are fine medieval bosses in the wagon roof. The north aisle is early 16th century. The capitals have carved foliage, vine leaves and grapes. One has a Green Man with leaves of artemisia. Another capital has a man in Tudor dress. The chancel, restored in 1845, has some medieval carving on the choir stalls and Bishop`s chair. The south transept is early 14th century and has a nave arch with fleurons. The east window of the transept is 14th century with a fragment of medieval glass. Puritans broke up the glass. Most windows in Perpendicular style are Victorian. There is some 16th century glass depicting four female saints in the east window of the north aisle. The tower is mid 15th century. The fan-vaulted porch is the work of Thomas Chard, born in the village in 1470, he later became the last abbot of Ford Abbey. It has a 'Bride`s Hand' in the stonework and the date 1708.

The Walk

From the car park cross the A373 with care to the lane opposite where there is a footpath sign. This lane goes over the little River Wolf. Caravans are in the nearby field in the summer. Go straight on in private grounds then turn left. A grassy path leads along the edge of the garden for 100 metres.

Turn right into a field and start climbing the hill. At first follow the hedge on the left. Then strike out to the furthest corner of the next field.

Cross over the brow of the hill and you look across cultivated fields and scattered trees of parkland above the River Otter. Veer left and go down to a stile. Keep on course southwest. Go under electric cables. You come down to a farm gate and stile, set in a corner off a remote lane.

Turn right and walk along the lane for ½ mile passing houses on the way. *The thatched buildings of Treaslake Farm are partly medieval. Their first residents may have attended the 'new' church up the hill in Buckerell.* We follow in their footsteps to the venerable church.

From Buckerell Church return down the hill past Treaslake Farm to the familiar farm gate on the left. **For the picturesque route,** retrace your steps over the hill to Awliscombe. Turn left to visit the Church.

For the flatter route along lanes: Pass the familiar farm gate and continue for ½ mile, southwest past Deer Park Farm on the right. Immediately after a bend in the road, turn left into Tape Lane enclosed with hedges. This unpaved track is used by horses that have stirred up the mud. A footbridge crosses the little River Wolf. The track leads to Weston Lane. Turn left to the nearby fork in the lane. Fork left and walk for ¼ mile back to the A373. Turn left for the Pub. Continue past the Pub to visit the Awliscombe Church.

4 Walks near Cullompton

Stone arch in Hunkin Wood

Walk 17: Plymtree to Clyst Hydon

Farms dominate the landscape in this fertile red sandstone country. Some doubtlessly have contributed to the beauty of their churches. Well signed footpaths take us over the fields.

Starting Point: The village sports field, just past the school, Plymtree.
Church **GR052028**   Sports Field **GR055029**   **Map:** OS Explorer 115
Terrain: Paths over fields and tracks, gently undulating   **Distance:** 6 Miles
Notes: 1.Cattle are in some fields. Avoid bringing a dog unless it is small enough to be carred. 2. The Plymtree Pub was closed at lunch time when we were there but the Community Shop around the corner was open.
3. Houses of Domesday and Elizabethan eras still stand in Plymtree Parish.

The Churches
The Parish Church of St John the Baptist, Plymtree is probably the first church built in this area, harking back to Saxon times. Plymtree became the Deanery Church for 15 parishes including Cullompton, Kentisbeare, Buckerell and Clyst Hydon. In the late 14th century the church was rebuilt in local stone, known as 'trap' and given a wagon roof of local oak. It was a simple church of nave and chancel. It would have been at the centre of village life. Fortunately the cloth trade brought wealth to the

Plymtree

Plymtree to Clyst Hydon

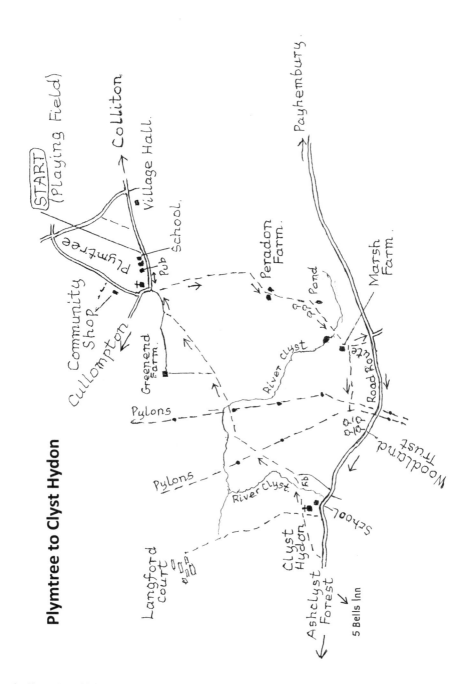

village. It is recorded that villagers paid for the 4 bells in the bell tower that was added in 1420. The Ford aisle was probably a private chapel, added in 15th century. A St Andrew's cross, recognised in the arms of Bishop Neville of Exeter (1448 – 1464), is carved on the capital of the arch joined to the wall. This detail helps point to the date of the new building. The porch was built at the same time and would have been the centre of local business. Plymtree has a very special rood screen, carved after 1470. It is outstanding in a county of fine screens. There is some original gilding. Panels at the lower part, have paintings of 34 saints. It contains the Stafford knot for Isabel, widow of Humphrey Stafford and also the Bourchier knot as she later married Sir Thomas Bourchier. (See Tawstock Church, Walk 5).

St Andrew`s Church, Clyst Hydon is approached via the front path. An ancient preaching cross faces the visitor. Halfway along this path an alehouse, the Refuge Inn, was said to have disturbed services. It is now a cottage. The name of the village suggests that there was a Norman church here. 'Clyst' is the name of the river and 'Hydon' derives from 'de Hidon'. The Norman church would have been contained in the central aisle. Its south wall was pierced in 15th century to form the south aisle. The pillars bear heraldic shields. The north aisle in a similar style was added in 19th century. The tower was built around 1400. It was partly rebuilt in 1657 when a piece of scaffolding stuck in the stonework where it remains. In 1832 the son of the schoolmaster, William Hole gave new pews to replace the battered seating.

Clyst Hydon

The Walk

Church and pub are neighbours in Plymtree. From the church entrance, cross to Greenend Lane opposite. Turn immediately left at footpath sign and head south on a track past houses then into fields.

The track becomes a footpath. Follow the hedge on the right then keep on course in the next field. There is a footpath sign in the field boundary and you can spy Peradon Farm over to the right. Head this way and go into the yard past farm buildings. You pass in front of the red brick farm house and emerge to an open field on your left.

Turn right and follow the hedgerow on the right. Go down to the field corner where a little wooden gate admits you to a copse. Pass a pond on the left and follow signs to an enclosed way to a large open field.

Cross diagonally left to a gate at Marsh Farm. The path on the south side of the farm crosses a stream to the farm track. Turn left. Keep straight on for the road route (see map). Otherwise, in 75 metres turn right into a large field.

For the field route turn right at footpath sign. Follow the hedge on the right. You are heading westwards towards pylons. Your hedge ends. Veer right to pick up another hedge. Follow this to go under the cables and pass solar panels. Make for the gate ahead into woodland.

There is a clearly marked path through this little copse, held by Woodland Trust. It brings you to a lane. Turn right for Clyst Hydon. You have an extra 1½ miles if you wish to visit the Five Bells Inn.

Just after the Village School, you come to the pathway to the Church.

From Clyst Hydon Church go to the gate at the back. You come to a remarkable 17th century house, 'Chelves Hayes'. Turn right here. In 50 metres at a corner of the drive there is a footpath tucked away beside a cottage. It leads to a small field and the tiny River Clyst. Take this path diagonally left to walk across footbridges to open fields.

At a path junction turn left and walk along a slightly elevated path heading northeast along the edge of the field. Go through a farmgate and keep on course towards pylons. They are ¼ mile apart. After the second pylon, cross another footbridge over the little river again.

Follow the hedge on the right. A flat footbridge takes you over a ditch. Continue northeast to cross a farm track. Keep straight on along the footpath uphill to a kissing gate. Plymtree can be seen ahead. Cross the narrow field to another kissing gate into Greenend Lane.

Turn right to return to the church. The community shop is to the left; the pub is to the right. Further on past the school is the sports field.

Walk 18: Kentisbeare to Saint Hill
(Cullompton a short drive away)

Quiet lanes and paths lead from a magnificent church to a humble Chapel

Starting Point: Kentisbeare Village Hall and Church Car Park   **GR068081**
Map: OS Explorer 115   **Terrain:** Gentle slopes and quiet ways
Distance: 4 ½ Miles
Note: nearby Cullompton on the other side of the motorway has a lovely church, described below and sadly not part of the walk.

The Churches
The Parish Church of St Mary, Kentisbeare has benefitted over the ages from skilled architects and great craftsmen in wood and stone who have come to give their best work. Generous donors have also been there at the right time. There are nine Domesday manors in the parish. The first church on this site was replaced in 14th century with a

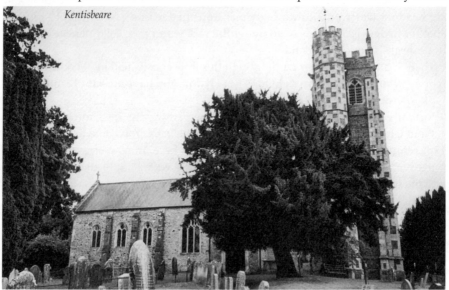

Kentisbeare

new, exquisite building in local stone. The chancel and tower survive. The tower is unique in Devon. The turret and buttresses have a chequer pattern of Beer stone and brown sandstone from Upton. Fierce heads jut out from the four top corners, they are the Beasts of the Apocalypse. The nave has some of the finest Perpendicular windows in Devon. Notice in particular the stonework of the north windows with their fleurons and heads probably of John and Anne Whiting in one of them and grotesque creatures in the other. The south aisle was added in the early 16th century thanks to the donation of a merchant venturer, John Whiting. It has four bays in the nave and a fifth in the

Kentisbeare to Saint Hill

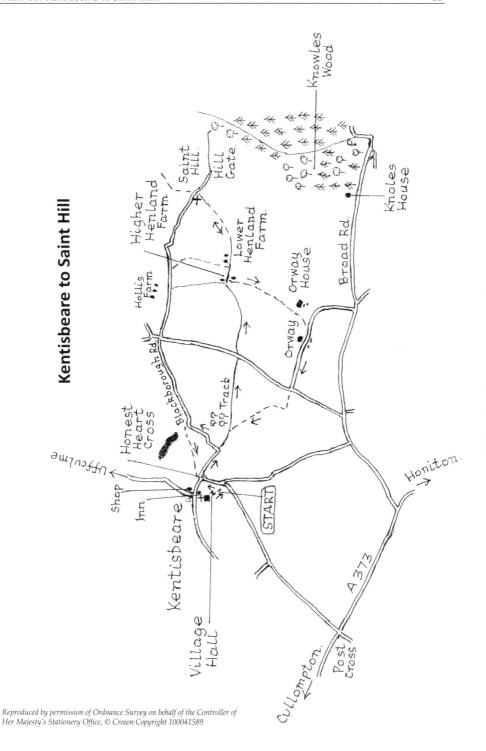

chancel. The capitals have various designs. The south Perpendicular windows are uniform apart from the most easterly. It contains some medieval glass. The east wall of the Whiting chapel has oak panels from Bradfield Hall a Devonshire mansion. A screen of the most delicate tracery stretches across the south aisle and the nave. It was probably the work of craftsmen from Tavistock Abbey. It has fan vaulting and the cornice still has original colours. Grapes, vines and leaves are among the carvings. There is much more in this church, including a link with Sir Walter Scott whose poem is on the north wall of the chancel. **Priesthall,** adjoining the churchyard is a perfect medieval church-house in cob and thatch.

Saint Hill Baptist Church is close to an ancient farm in a remote hamlet. Its chief charm is the quiet contemplation of the fertile Devonshire fields that roll up to its graveyard.

Cullompton, St Andrew escaped a fire that burnt down 200 houses in this once flourishing cloth town. The church is entirely Perpendicular in style. The tower was built between 1545 and 1549, a little later than the main body. According to Arthur Mee, 'The purple red stone of its church tower rises over 100 feet, impressive with its eight pinnacles, its richly carved niches, its traceried belfry windows and a Crucifixion scene crumbling away after about four centuries. This lovely tower is 16th century and leads us into a church which was here 100 years before it'. The red stone is local and the carvings are in Beer and Ham Hill stone. The church has a rare clerestory and a wagon

Cullompton

roof stretching above nave and chancel with angel corbels. It has 144 panels, each with a carved boss in the centre. Wall plates have vine decoration. There are six bays and north and south aisles. The piers are tall and thin. The fan-vaulted 'Lane Aisle' is quite famous. John Lane, a cloth merchant started it in 1526 and died in 1529. He intended it as his chantry chapel. 32 men in Tudor costume can be seen on the piers. Some of the buttresses between the large windows have symbols of his trade: ships, cloth shears, teasel frames. The 15th century screen is one of the longest in Devon. It has 11 bays, 3 to each aisle and 5 to the nave. A fearsome golgotha once stood above the rood screen. A statue of Christ crucified would have been on top. The chancel has been well restored by Edward Ashworth in mid 19th century. It has a large Perpendicular east window.

The Walk

In Kentisbeare, walk back up to the entrance to the spacious car park. Turn left to walk on the raised verge to the nearby crossroads, 'Honest Heart Cross'. Turn right into Backborough Lane (no road signs)..

After ¼ mile of narrow hedged lane, keep straight on into a traffic free **track**. You are heading eastwards on a fairly foot friendly path. Avoid the path on the right (we shall return that way).

In under ½ mile you come to a lane* at a junction. Cross to the tarmac farm track opposite, a fairly elevated path to Higher Henland Farms. **Note** the cross paths here for the return walk. Continue heading eastwards to Lower Henland Farm. Soon after this farm turn left to a footpath into a field.

Cross the field diagonally right to the far corner where you pick up the track to Saint Hill. Pass a cottage or two and you find the Baptist Chapel on a corner of the access lane. *Go to the back of the chapel for views over the countryside you have passed on your walk.*

If you wish to head for the wooded hills shown on the map, turn right on the lane and continue eastwards (see the map).

To return from Saint Hill to Kentisbeare, return across the field to Lower Henland Farm and retrace you steps to Upper Henland Farm and the cross paths. Turn left into a muddy field entrance. Head south on the narrow bumpy verge with the hedge on your left at first. In the second field, cut across to the left corner, then go through to the third field where the path is enclosed. Only the barns of Orway House can be seen on the left. The path swings to the right to come to the road.

Turn right and pass Orway Farm. In ¼ mile, at the T-junction with the same *lane at a lower point, cross to a footpath. Keep on course as far as the boundary hedge. Turn right to follow the hedge and go through a gate into the next spacious field. Cross northwestwards up over a hillock and down to a field corner. *As you cross you have a view over the lake on the right.*

At the final field follow the hedge on the left and come out at the original **track**. Retrace your steps to the end of the track. *Keep straight on for the nearer route. At Honest Heart Cross, turn right for Kentisbeare.*

Otherwise, turn right to walk down Blackborough Road for ¼ mile. At a bend in the road turn left into woodland. The path leads through this copse then veers right uphill. Look behind you for a view of the nearby lake. In the next elevated field the path has been moved to the edge. It is a bumpy overgrown path and walkers have tended to tread the smoother surface close to the crop.

A bungalow is ahead. Pass this on the drive and you come to Kentisbeare, halfway up Priests Hill. Turn right and walk down to the crossroads. The village shop is on your right, the inn is on your left and then the Church.

After Visiting Kentisbeare Church, climb through the churchyard to the south side and enjoy a completely different aspect from the Car Park.

Walk 19: Uffculme to Spiceland to Culmstock

*Below the Blackdown Hills the little River Culm links villages where the churches have presided
for a thousand years*

Starting Point: At the bottom of Bridge Street, Uffculme, the footpath runs along a back
lane with limited parking **GR069126 Map:** OS Explorer 128 **Distance:** 7 Miles **Terrain:**
riverside meadows, wood, one hill, some roads
Local Information: 1. Uffculme was granted permission to hold a market in 1266. The
Village Square 'the Shambles' was the site of successive markets.
2. Culmstock was once a wool town. The old mill and 18th century weavers` cottages
are near the river. Its population was much greater then.
3. Hunkin Wood is managed by the Woodland Trust. The planting of new trees,
including Hazel, is part of the Culm Valley Millenium Project.
4. The old railway line ran 1876–1975 from Hemyock to Tiverton Junction. It served the
dairy factory at Hemyoke and also carried passengers. Much of the track was beside the
River Culm. Trains maintained a maximum speed of 15 m.p.h.

The Churches
Note: On weekdays Uffculme Church is open during school term time.

   Uffculme, St Mary the Virgin stands on the corner of the Square of this old wool
town. Little remains of the original 12th century church. Inside, the round pillars of the

Uffculme   *Culmstock*

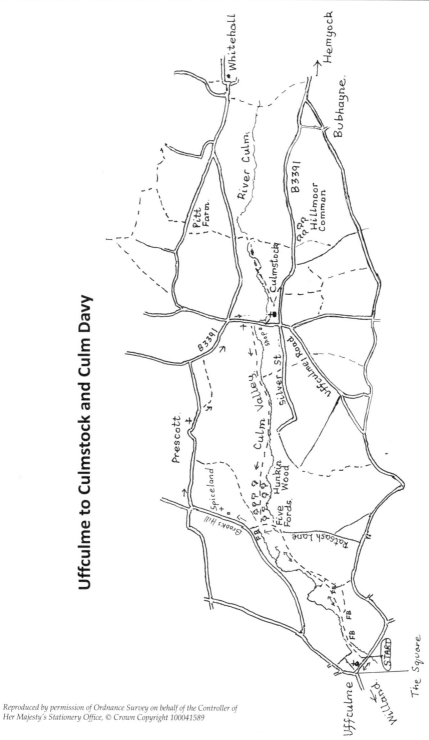

Uffculme to Culmstock and Culm Davy

three-bay arcade to the north aisle date from 13th century. The east end of the arcade and the south aisle are Perpendicular. The 15th century screen, at 67 feet, is the longest in Devon. It has fan vaulted coving on both sides. Some of the original green and red colours have been restored.

Beyond the screen, two chapels are on either side of the sanctuary. The Walrond chapel on the north holds a large tomb of 1663. The Brice Chapel on the south is named after an organist. The table in front of the screen is used for services in the nave. The medieval tower has a Victorian spire.

Spiceland, the Quaker Meeting House was first built in this secluded spot in 17th century. It was replaced in 1815 by the present cottage-like building and retains all the features, including seating of that period. It is a place of peace.

Baptist Chapel, Prescott dates from 1785. It has a gallery, baptistry and barrel-vaulted ceiling.

Culmstock, All Saints rises above the River Culm. The Manor belonged to the Bishops of Exeter in 1086. 'Roger was priest of Culmstock in 1175'. The chancel is believed to date from 1200 but has been drastically restored. Most of the church: nave, south aisle, font and porch date from 1300. Ralph de Culmstock became Prior of Taunton Priory in 1326. John Prescott (from the hamlet we passed) was probably buried in the Lady Chapel in 1412. Masses would have been said for him. This chapel, now the South Aisle, had a squint into the chancel to enable the chaplain to co-ordinate with the priest at the High Altar. The missing squint was discovered in 1911. Perhaps the greatest restoration damage was to the ancient stone rood screen. It has been ripped out and broken so that some is in the tower and some forms a reredos. On the plus side, the clerestory added in 1820, adds light and height to the building. The acoustics here have been praised. The church houses a treasure that escaped the Reformation; 'the Culmstock Cope', embroidered in 1400s, was restored in 1980 and is under cover in the north aisle. More famous is the yew tree growing on the medieval tower!

The Walk

Walk along the back lane, Dennersway for ¼ mile to a footbridge. Cross to meadowland and follow the River Culm on your left. Glimpse through trees to the river. In another ¼ mile a footbridge leads to another wide meadow.

The river curves to the left. Cut across the curve following a hedge on the right. Cross another footbridge and rejoin the river as it curves back to meet you. Keep going to the next meadow and once again the river curves to the left. Cut across to another point where the 'unmetalled road', Ratsash Lane leads off to the right. Avoid this turning and follow the river round towards Hunkin Wood.

Here an intriguing little gate welcomes you. Cross the green swathe to a footbridge. Footpaths lead off to the right and we may come back on one of them. Meanwhile head for the seat and an information board on the wood.

Pass these on the right and you find that you are close to a lane. *Uffculme is to the left.* Turn right and climb Brooks Hill, passing a complex of stables. Then you come to the Quaker Meeting House, Spicelands. *Here time stands still. The gardener has put down his fork and the sweet peas wave their heads over the vegetables. The ginger cat comes to see what you are about on the seat where you view the serene countryside. Heaven!*

From Spicelands return to the lane and continue north to crossroads at Lower Cross.

Turn right and walk down a lane heading east. Pass a farm at Prescott, then a track on the right *leading back to Hunkin Wood*. Continue eastwards past the Baptist Meeting House that shares its graveyard with the neighbouring house. In another 50 metres turn right.

A view opens to the hills as you join a footpath over a sloping field. Veer left and hug the hedgerow opposite until you find a stile into the next field. Turn left so the hedge is on your left. Pass a farmhouse on your right and you come out on the B3391, Prescott Road. Turn right to follow the road down to Culmstock. *There is a speed limit, we did not find traffic too bad.*

As you walk down to the river that is central to Culmstock, you pass the Methodist Chapel on the right and the Pub on the left. **The footpath** back to Uffculme is on the right, just before the bridge. The shop-cum-café is on the other side of the river. Climb a little further up 'Town Hill' and veer left along the 'Cleeve' for the Church.

For the walk back to Uffculme, return to the bridge and cross to the marked footpath now on your left. Below, on the river bank you have a good view of the handsome stone bridge. With your back to the bridge, follow an enclosed path heading west beside the river. It leads to open meadows.

Do not be tempted over the footbridge but enjoy a delightful walk on flat meadows beside the river on your left. *A lush hedge of alder trees grows along the far bank of the river that seems wider here. The shy otter may have his home here.*

After the first meadow you have a short walk along the old railway line that runs parallel to the river. In the next meadow veer away from the old railway bridge and find footpath signs over to the right. They direct you through the ragged hedge and back to the river. You pass a pebbly beach with low cliffs. Go through another loose hedge and make for Hunkin Wood seen ahead. Just inside the wood there is a stone arch and a poem attached.

Either continue on the riverside path or follow footpath signs through the wood. You come to the familiar grassy swathe with the seat up on the right. Turn left to recross the footbridge and open the intriguing little gate back to meadows. Turn right and retrace your steps back to Uffculme.

Spiceland

Walk 20: Bickleigh to Tiverton

A straightforward riverside walk from a village church to a busy cathedral-like centre in a once wealthy Devonshire town. Return by bus.

Starting Point: Bickleigh Church. Parking at Village Hall.   GR942072
Map: OS Explorer 114   **Terrain:** Flat, riverside, wet after rain. One steep climb up to Bickleigh Church   **Distance:** 4½ Miles Walk, 4 Miles Bus
Local Information: Bus 55 plies between Tiverton and Exeter every ½ hour (2 hourly on Sunday) stops at Bickleigh.   Phone Traveline 01392 42 77 11
Bickleigh Bridge spanning the River Exe with 5 arches was built in 1630.
Bickleigh Mill is now an arts centre and café near Devon Railway Centre
Exe Valley Way from the Exe Estuary to Exford on Exmoor is 50 miles long. Our section on footpaths stays mainly close to the river.
Tiverton's Museum is in Beck's Square, open weekdays, closed Sundays.
Tourist Information Centre is now in the Museum, phone 01884 230878

The Churches
St Peter's Church, Tiverton stands near the site of a timber Saxon Church. The Saxon 'Twyfiride', meaning 'two fords' reflects the town's position between two

Tiverton

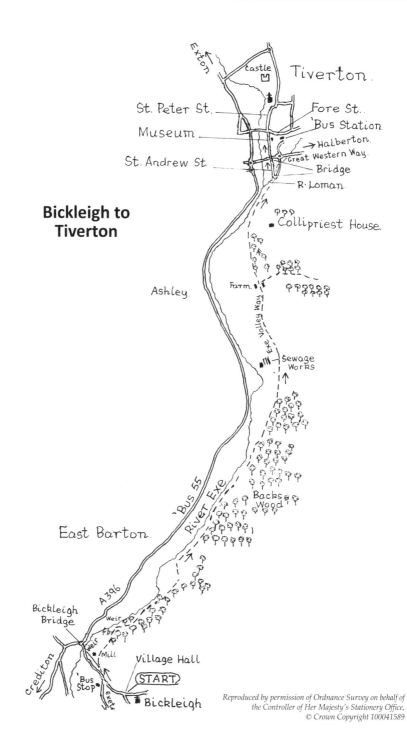

Bickleigh to Tiverton

rivers, the Exe and the Loman. The manor was held by Gytha, the Mother of King Harold. She tried in vain to repel the forces of William the Conqueror. The Normans won and rebuilt the Church. It was consecrated in 1073 by Bishop Leofric of Exeter. From that period only the Norman doorway with dog tooth and chevron carving remains to be seen, on the outside from the castle side. In 13th century the Courtenays held the Manor and the Castle. They spent their energies on the Wars of the Roses. Meanwhile the new merchant class looked after the town and the church. The chancel arcade and 99 foot high tower with eight pinnacles date from the early 15th century. The tower has been buttressed to protect it from the River Exe. In the early 16th century merchants rebuilt the south aisle and added a porch. Here a rare carving of the Virgin Mary reminds us that she was important to Drapers. John Greenway, a merchant adventurer and self-made man had the porch and chantry chapel built. As you approach the Church, you see the contrast between their light Beer stone and the dark red of the tower. The windows of the Chantry Chapel are Perpendicular. Outside, above the windows are carvings of ships. Above the ships are carvings depicting the life of Christ. The original 16th century door gives access to the grand Chapel. The ceiling was renewed in 1826. Two brasses of John and Joan Greenway have been lifted from the floor to the wall where they make an impact. The Victorians have rebuilt the rest of this spacious church. The stained glass of the east and west windows is by Wailes. The east window in celestial blue amd white is particularly beautiful. An ornate font by Harbottle (1909) replaces an older one. Repair and refurbishment continue today.

Parish Church of St Mary the Virgin, Bickleigh is high on a steep lane. The late

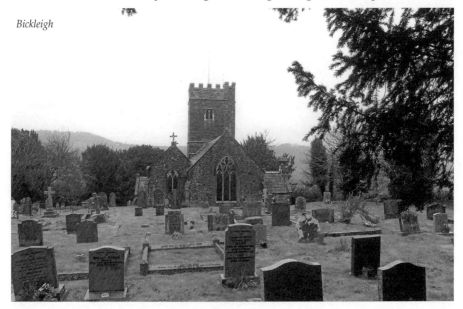

Bickleigh

12th century font is the oldest item; it is tub shaped with star and pellet carving around the top. The church was consecrated in 1268 and the tower survives from that period. The south aisle was added in 15th century. It has four arches and carved capitals. The most easterly has the leafy face of a green man. Tombs of the Carew family are here. One is of Elizabeth who died when her son was only two. Another is of Bampfylde Moore Carew, well born in 1693. He ran away to join the gypsies, became a trickster, was arrested and escaped in America. Back in England, he became known as 'King of the Beggars'. Among the bench ends, the one facing you as you enter depicts a man with the tools of the wool trade. The Victorians rebuilt much of the church in Decorated style.

The Walk

The Village Hall Car Park is just below the Church. After visiting Bickleigh Church, walk down past this Car Park to the bottom of the hill and turn right to Bickleigh Mill.

Turn right before the Mill so that you pass it on your left. You have joined the Exe Valley Way and look out for signs   .

Go to the back of the Mill then follow a stream at the edge of a field towards woodland. Enter the wood where a muddy path runs beside the river. It descends to the river and you will find a permissive path by the river leading over a ditch to to an open field. Here is a private suspension bridge.

Keep on course to further woodland. Walk beside the river through Backs Wood for 1 mile. Emerge to a field and cross a ditch. The sewage works are ahead. Pass these on your left.

You now join a track for over a mile, passing Collipriest Farm then Collipriest House. Over to your right is the Iron Age settlement, Cranmore Castle

At a road junction turn left into St Andrew Street. It crosses first the River Loman then The Great Western Way on a footbridge. You are now in Tiverton. The Museum is on your right and the Bus Station is ahead. (See notes above).

Catch the 55 (Exeter Bus) and ask for the stop after Bickleigh Bridge. When you alight from the bus, walk up the hill, following the lane on your left. Pass Bickleigh Mill on your left and continue climbing to the Village Hall Car Park.

8 Walks near Exeter

Walk 21: East Budleigh to Bicton Park and Otterton

A varied walk from a Devonshire village to a church in a theme park and back along the River Otter, after a visit to a water mill and tea rooms

Starting Point: In front of Village Hall Stores, East Budleigh **GR**066848
          Or Hayes Lane Car Park, East Budleigh   **GR**065848
Map: OS Explorer 115   **Terrain:** Fairly Flat   **Distance:** 5 Miles
Local Information: 1. East Budleigh was known as Bodelie in Domesday. It was an important port before the River Otter silted up in 15th century. There are cob and thatch houses. Walter Raleigh was born at Hayes Barton, a Tudor house at the end of Hayes Lane.
2. Bicton Park is open all year round (£8) and has botanical gardens and a palm house. It also has a miniature railway, Play area and mini golf. The church is kept locked except for services. The Obelisk of 1747 was a landmark for the Rolles family who owned the estate from 17th century.
3. Otterton has a working water mill, restored in 1977. It also has a bakery, tearooms and gift shop. In the Main Street a house is dated 1627.

The Churches
All Saints, East Budleigh. Saxon stones have been found in one of the walls of this

East Budleigh

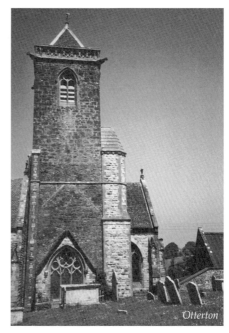
Otterton

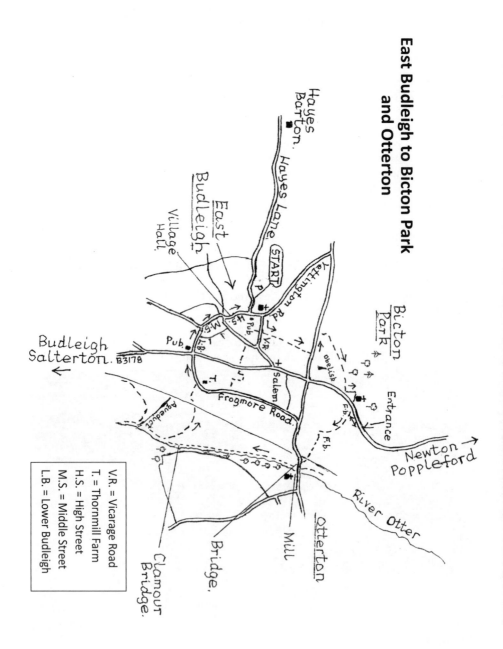

East Budleigh to Bicton Park and Otterton

V.R. = Vicarage Road
T. = Thornmill Farm
H.S. = High Street
M.S. = Middle Street
L.B. = Lower Budleigh

church. This thriving Saxon village no doubt had a church then. There was a Priory near the Manor of 'Budley Polso' as it was called in 12th century. The nuns took good care of the church for 350 years. The church consisted of tower, nave and chancel. The walls had bright frescoes. Bishop Lacy enlarged the church in 1420. It now had south and north aisles and the tower gained two upper stages. The medieval wagon roof has a variety of 15th century bosses, repainted in 1974. At the Dissolution in 1540 the nuns were expelled from All Saints. The Manor passed through many hands. Under Edward V1 and Elizabeth 1, in a campaign against Popish practices, the church lost its money, its rood and its altar. The rood staircase was hidden behind rubble and uncovered in 1891. Stained glass was broken under Cromwell. One window has survived unscathed; the east window of the north aisle has old glass bearing the arms of Bishop Lacy. Revd Ambrose Stapleton, vicar for 59 years from 1794 has a memorial in the east window of the south aisle. 63 delightful carved oak bench ends bring to life the experiences of ordinary men in 16th century and express their humour. They have no religious theme. Walter Raleigh, born at Hayes Barton in 1552, went to church here as a youngster.

Bicton, St Mary is an unusual grey Victorian building, built in memory of her husband by Lady Louisa Rolle in 1850. It is cruciform church designed by Hayward in Decorated style. It has brilliant stained glass windows. Many sculptured heads support the roof inside. More heads are in the chancel.

The Mausoleum, Bicton was the original estate church. It has been transformed into a picturesque medieval ruin with the aid of Pugin.

Otterton, St Michael and All Angels. Only the tower survives from the Medieval church. The rest was rebuilt in Decorated style in 1870. Otterton has a rich history. The Countess Gythia, mother of King Harold owned the Manor and fought against William the Conqueror`s army at Exeter. She fled to Flanders. William gave the Manor to the Benedictine Abbey of Mont St Michel. A Priory was built here in 12th century. The monks seem to have rebuilt the Saxon church for the villagers and added a nave west of the tower for themselves so that there were two sections to the church. They even cut a way through the tower to reach their gardens. Above the north arch of the tower are the remains of a Norman window. Their tenants had to contribute to the Prior, buying him a palfrey and supplying the best fish to him. The Priory fell to ruin after 1415 when Henry V suppressed foreign monasteries. Local landowners supported the church but this building too had deteriorated so far by mid- 19th century, that it was demolished. The new church of Beer stone has marble pillars. The reredos of Caen stone is from Normandy. The tower is at the east end.

The Walk
Walk uphill on the High Street to East Budleigh Church. From All Saints cross with care to residential Vicarage Road. In 300 metres turn left into an insignificant footpath between houses to the playing field.

Keep to the hedge on the left heading northeast. In 500 metres you reach the lane to Yettington. An obelisk is to the right.

Bicton

Turn left and walk along the lane for about 220 metres. Just past a farm opening on the left, turn right into a field footpath. Follow the field boundary on the right for 75 metres. Then turn right onto a track. Pass woodland on the left and obelisk on the right. Just before the main road turn left into a track between walls to Bicton Park. All gates are locked. You can view the church behind bars then take the narrow alley to the main road, B3178.

Turn left then cross to the footpath under trees opposite. Immediately on the left, a footbridge leads to a path to the entrance to Bicton Park. Otherwise go straight on.

From Bicton Park (if you decide to go there), return to the sheltered path and turn left to continue under trees. The path follows a stream on the left. Cross the old railway then a long footpath over another stream. You now reach the road to Otterton. Turn left and cross the road bridge over the River Otter. *The Mill on the right offers refreshments, baked bread and gifts to tempt you, not to mention an opportunity to watch the waterwheel at work*

To visit the church, continue towards the village, along Fore St. Turn right up Church Hill.

From Otterton Church, return to cross the road bridge and turn immediately left into the path beside the river. This is a pleasant path beside clear sparkling water, overhung with trees. It heads south towards Budleigh Salterton but we stop short in 1 kilometre at Clamour Bridge on the left. Turn right into a path across the meadow to East Budleigh. A low aqueduct can be seen on the left.

You cross the old railway again and come out on Frogmore Road at Thornmill Farm, the site of another watermill. Continue ahead to cross B3178 and follow village streets, Lower Budleigh, Middle Street and High Street. You may be able to help yourself to tea or coffee at the Village Hall.

Walk 22: Donkey Sanctuary to Branscombe & Salcombe Regis (fig. of 8)

From base you head east to Branscombe, a National Trust village on the coast or west to Salcombe Regis. Both walks include valleys down to the sea.

Starting Point: The Donkey Sanctuary **GR**161892 **Map:** OS Explorer 115
Terrain: Flat inland, steep coastal paths **Distances:** Walk 1: 7 Miles
Walk 2: 4 Miles

Local Information: 1. The Donkey Sanctuary, just south of A3052 is well signed and offers free parking, a visitor centre and a restaurant. It also provides some grass tracks, a refuge from the lanes. It was founded in 1969 by Elizabeth Svendson and relies on donations. The extraordinary generosity of donors can be seen in the huge acreage and first class facilities.

2. Edge Barton is the medieval birthplace of Bishop Branscombe (1280). It had a chapel and there are the remains of a round 14th century window. Much of the house is Tudor.

3. Hole, recorded in 1249, is now a compact house built in chequer and flint c.1600. It looks down the valley seawards. The ruins of an earlier building lie in the front garden.

4. National Trust properties in Branscombe include The Old Bakery, where teas are served late March to early November 10.30 – 5, Wednesday to Sunday. In summer it opens every day. Phone 01927 680481

The Churches

The Church of Saint Winifred, Branscombe may be the burial place of the Celtic St Brannock or Branwallader. Dedication to the early Saxon martyr, Saint Winifred is unusual. Some Saxon stones have been found in the fabric of the church. No other vestige survives of the church believed to have existed then. In 925 A.D. the Manor was given to the Benedictine Monastery of St Peter, Exeter. The church is hidden from the sea by cliffs and woodland. Was this site chosen to avoid Danish looters? The early days are intriguing. By contrast, successive stages in building development are quite clear. The central tower and part of the nave are Norman. In 13th century the transepts were added not to the tower, as the stair turret was in the way, but to the nave. The north transept has a piscina for washing vessels, a niche and an aumbrey or cupboard for vessels and books. The south transept was the Priest`s Chapel. The nave was lengthened westwards in 13th century. Bishop Walter Bronescombe, (see Note 2 above) may have overseen these enlargements. In 14th century the round arches were redesigned. The pointed replacements are too heavy for the slender capitals and shafts. The south transept was given a splendid Decorated window. The north transept kept its ordinary lancet. As windows grew bigger they let light into the original gloom. The chancel is early 14th century with windows to match. The low shuttered windows would have allowed lepers from

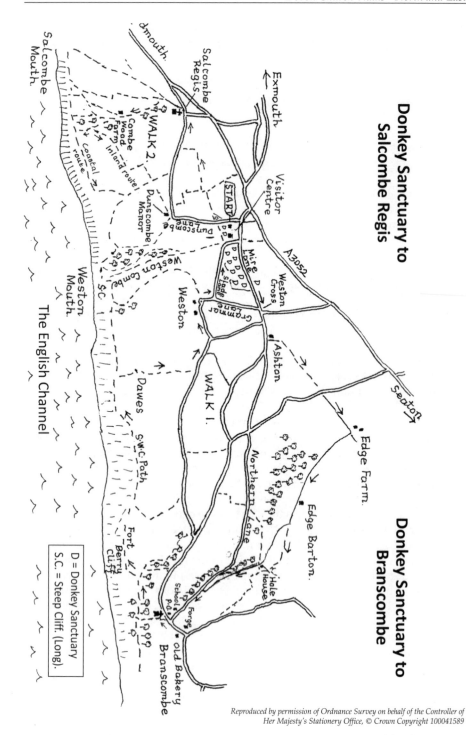

Donkey Sanctuary to Salcombe Regis

Donkey Sanctuary to Branscombe

D = Donkey Sanctuary
S.C. = Steep Cliff. (Long).

Branscombe

the outside to observe mass inside. Grandest of all in best Beer stone, was the addition in 15th century of the fine five-light east window. It bears the arms of George Neville, Bishop of Exeter (1458-64). During the Reformation, John Tailor, an anti-Papist was vicar here (1539-40). The church`s stained glass, sedilia, piscina, canopies and murals were spoilt in the frenzy of Puritan destruction. In a reversal of fortune, Tailor himself was burned at the stake in1555. On to happier times, the gallery was added in 16th century. It has oak panels with fleur de lys carvings and Tudor roses below. Musicians and possibly the benefactor and his family would sit here. Outside stone steps lead to this gallery. Carved oak altar rails were made in 1660. The chancel screen was added to an existing base. The unusual three- tier pulpit is late 18th century. In 1911 the decaying church was saved by W. D. Caroe`s extensive restoration. The Millenium cross in local stone is by Stephen Budd.

The Church of St Mary and St Peter, Salcombe Regis stands in a quiet cemetery looking down the lovely valley to the sea. As at Branscombe the manor was given to the Monastery of Exeter in the 920s with no record of a church. Early in the 12th century a stone church was built here but little remains of that Norman building. Some stone work in the walls, a round pillar in the north aisle and one small lancet in the southwest have survived. In 13th century the north arcade and aisle, the south arcade and aisle also the chancel arch were added. In 1258 Bishop Branscombe dedicated the church to the Virgin Mary. Then came a period of devastation in 14th century when the Plague depleted the population. The church fabric suffered; the chancel had no roof. Books and vestments suffered. Unable to find workmen for the fields, farmers turned to sheep farming. Wool provided a good income and the church also benefited. In 15th century the church was repaired and enlarged. High

Salcombe Regis

wagon roofs were installed. The north aisle still has its original roof. New, larger windows gave more light. In 1445 the Perpendicular tower was built in 3 stages. In 1450 Bishop Lacey rededicated the church to St Mary and St Peter. The chancel Early English east window was removed in 19th century and carefully replaced. The north aisle Decorated window has fragments of 15th century glass. The Perpendicular south aisle window was damaged in the War and now has clear glass. The Millennium gift to this church is the Altar triptych, designed and started by Lawrence Whistler and finished by his son, Simon.

The Walk

Part 1 to Branscombe

From the Donkey Sanctuary Car Park walk out onto Branscombe Road and turn right to nearby crossroads and turn right into Mire Lane. Walk straight on to <u>Weston Cross</u>. **Or** *you can reach Mire Lane by going behind the Visitor Centre, past the restaurant and following Walk B for about 75 metres. (You leave Walk B when it crosses Mire Road. You turn right to walk along the road to <u>Weston Cross</u>).*

Keep straight on to nearby house, Ashton Farm. Just past the house, turn left into a track. Pass the house again on your left then turn right, following the track north eastwards. In ¼ mile pass a farm building and keep straight on across fields with the hedge on your right. In ¼ mile you come to a byway. Keep on course by crossing to a no-through-road opposite.

Edge Farm, under conversion at the moment, is at the end of this road. Turn right here and continue ¼ mile down on the track to Edge Barton. Here you have entered another century where a few timeless cottages overlook the beautiful valley leading down to the sea. The footpath veers to the right of the ancient manor house and follows the stream down to woodland.

Soon after entering the trees, you turn right avoiding the damp field path ahead. There are enough mud patches on our more elevated track! It climbs to go along the edge of Hole Hill. There are views across the valley to Woodhouse away to the left.

At Hole you reach another handsome historic home (See above). It faces south and we follow the driveway in that direction for 1 kilometre. Soon after passing Branscombe Primary School, you come to a T-junction.

The Old Bakery and Forge are to the left (see Note 4 above). The Post Office and Church are to the right. Walk up to Branscombe Church. As you approach, you see a finger post pointing to the footpath down as far as the tower where you veer left into undergrowth in the dank churchyard.

Cross a footbridge over a stream and start climbing. Keep to the right hand side of a small field. Woodland is on your right and up ahead. Wild garlic has taken over the woodland floor. When you enter the wood, veer left and keep climbing to a T-junction. You have reached the South West Coast Path. Turn right. You have the luxury of a firm, flat dry path through the trees.

After ¼ mile you leave the track signposted to Fountain Head. Turn left and climb past old quarries to the cliff top. Here you have the joy of open, flatish fields high above the sea on your left. *Fulmars may be seen floating above the cliffs. You are on Berry Cliffs and pass prehistoric earthworks on your right.* In 500 metres at a path junction, stick to the coastal path. You see some cottages ahead to the right and can cross a wide field diagonally towards them. Go through to the next field where you are at the head of a valley. *There is a path to the left down to the sea.* Cross the valley to climb to the cliff top ahead. Here are more flat fields sheltered by rough hedge on the left cutting out the sea view. You come to a kissing gate and information board.

Turn right here and head north towards a lone cottage, 'Daws'. Pass the cottage on your right and continue northwards on the driveway. In 1 kilometre from the coast you emerge onto the road to Weston.

Turn left towards that hamlet. Pass a lane on the right and you reach the farm cottages that make up Weston. Follow Grammar Lane round to the right to the junction with Slade Lane. Cross to a gap in the hedge on this corner. You have re-entered the outer realms of the Donkey Sanctuary. Follow the grass verge that runs parallel to Slade Lane on your left. This is Walk C and will lead you back to the Visitor Centre and Car Park.

Part 2 to Salcombe Regis

Leave the Donkey Sanctuary by the main entrance and cross the lane diagonally left to a signed footpath into a flat field. The path heads southwestwards and has a fence on the right.

In ¼ mile at cross paths turn left. The sign pointing to Salcombe Regis is misleading. So **Stop!** Turn immediately right to keep on course in the next field for

South Devon Scenes

another ¼ mile. Now you turn sharp left to find the lane to Salcombe Regis.

Turn right on the lane and walk down past cottages to the Church at crossroads. Turn left so that you pass the church and walk down on a lane sign-posted to the sea. Pass the Church Car Park on the left. You are heading south and *the shortest route to the sea continues on the footpath down through fields in the valley* but I have chosen an easier route back.

Veer left on the tarmac road up to Combe Wood Farm. Go past thatched cottages then head left to climb more steeply on a well defined path. There are extensive views over the valley. In 250 metres you have another choice:

1. **For the gentler route back to the Donkey Sanctuary,** turn left on the firm generous gentle slope through woodland. Emerge at elevated fields. Follow the hedge on the left through two fields with mud patches near their entrances. Turn left just before a barn and head north with a field on your right. At the field corner there is a lone house on the other side of the hedge, Turn right again to walk along another edge of the field to cross paths.*

Coastal walkers join the path here and turn right.

Keep straight on to walk on a tarmac track. Go through gates and continue on the track to the end where it veers left to pass Dunscombe Manor House and holiday park on the right.

When you reach the lane, turn right and follow it round a bend to a large shed. Here you can re-enter the grounds of the Donkey Sanctuary and take the grass track running parallel to the lane. There are many donated seats here for picnickers to view the donkeys and enjoy the tranquility. Follow the seats back to the Donkey Sanctuary.

2. **For the more challenging coastal route back to the Donkey Sanctuary** avoid the gentle sloping path on the left. Keep straight on to clamber through a tree's roots. A narrow path soon veers left up the hillside where you have a scramble up over lumpy slopes to join the South West Coast Path. Turn left.

You are on Higher Dunscombe Cliff overlooking the open sea. Keep to the cliff top for over ¼ mile when the coast path turns inland and slopes downhill.

Take the first path to the left to join the easier route 1. Above*.

(If you go right down to Weston Mouth for a swim, **beware** the shelving of the beach may make leaving the water difficult and there may be nudists! Leave the Coast Path before it crosses the stream and takes the long haul up Weston Cliff).

Red sandstone and cream greensand used to be quarried. The quarries were reopend on 1979 for repair to Exeter Cathedral.

Walk 23: Topsham to Exeter

From an ancient port, take a short ferry ride and a longer walk beside canal and River Exe to Exeter. Return on foot, by bus or most scenically by train.

Starting Point: Topsham Railway Station   **GR**967884
Map: OS Explorer 114 **Terrain:** Flat, riverside   **Distance:** 7 Miles one way
Local Information: 1. Topsham – Exminster Ferry operates weekends off-season and daily April to Sepember. I found the ferry closed Tuesdays in May when you would have to walk on the east bank. Phone 07801 203338
2. Topsham was the main port of the area even before the Romans came. In 1282 the Countess of Devon built a weir across the Exe to prevent Exeter from having the trade, mainly in wool. In 1566 the first lock canal was built linking Exeter with the Estuary. Topsham merchants brought back brick from Holland and built houses in the Strand in the Dutch style, 1700-25. The wool trade diminished. In 19th century Topsham went into boat building and rope making. It retains riverside views and Georgian merchant houses.
3. Exeter`s town walls are Roman but the city only began to flourish under Alfred the Great. It became a centre for the wool industry and exported woven cloth from quays on the River Exe. Silverware and pottery were also made and traded here. There are six medieval churches in central Exeter and walking tours are available, 11 a.m.- 2 p.m.   Phone 01392 265203
4. Bus 57 from Exeter Bus Station to Topsham runs frequently
       Phone Traveline 0871200 2223

The Churches

St Margaret`s Church, Topsham has fine views over the Exe Estuary. A church at Topsham is first mentioned in 1295. Crusaders returning to England probably brought with them the legend of St Margaret of Antioch, beheaded for her faith. Unfortunately the main body of the church was destroyed by fire in 1676. Only the tower survived. It is built of red sandstone, suggesting a Medieval church of that material. The battlemented top of the tower was raised in 1877 to make room for a chiming clock. The Victorians built the present spacious church in pale limestone in 1874-6. The font has a Norman carving of a dragon.

Topsham

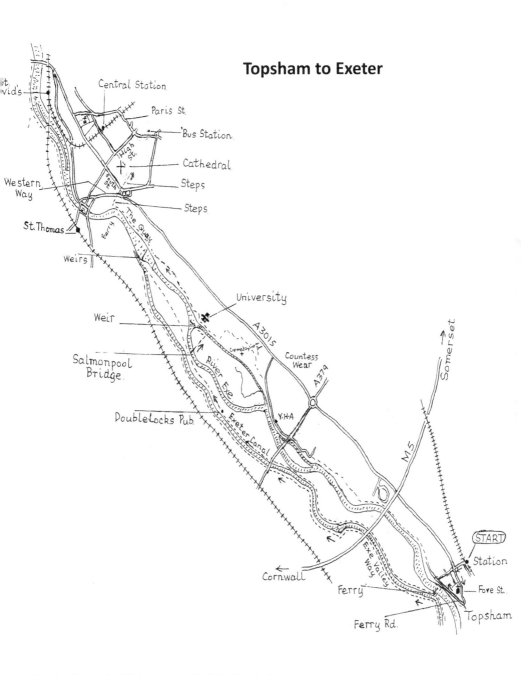

Topsham to Exeter

Reproduced by permission of Ordnance Survey on behalf of the Controller of
Her Majesty's Stationery Office, © Crown Copyright 100041589

The Cathedral of St Peter, Exeter takes its dedication from the Benedictine Monastery that was here from 7th century. In 1050 Leofric was made Bishop of Exeter in the monastery church. This building was then neglected when the Normans built a grand new church in 1112, under the patronage of William Warelwast, nephew of the Conqueror. The Norman Church in turn was completely remodelled 1275 – 1369. The two great towers were retained and made to open onto the new transepts. The east end and the nave were demolished to be replaced with a great length of stone magnificence in three stage ordonnance. Succeeding bishops contributed to this building to create a consistently Decorated cathedral. The longest vaulted ceiling in the world has been

compared to an avenue of trees. It has 374 fine bosses. The Lady Chapel of 1279 contains the tomb of Bishop Branscombe who died in 1280. The designers of the east window were ahead of their time in the Decorated style. The chapter house on the south side was restored in 1969. Outside, the

Exeter

Photos: Exeter Cathedral

Exeter

west front has a Gothic screen with three tiers of statues, most famous are the seated monarchs who wave their royal hands in different gestures. Above the screen the grand Decorated window has a pentagonal star in the tracery. The stones in Exeter Cathedral lead up to Heaven. They have been quarried in conditions described as 'Hell'. Local Beer stone is used for intricate carvings in the roof and the front. The coarser yellow Salcombe stone was also used in building the Cathedral in 14th and 15th centuries. .

The Walk

Walk down Station Road a few paces into town and turn left into Fore Street. Follow the road past shops to the nearby St Margaret`s Church on the right. From the church tower go down steps to Ferry Road. Turn right.

Pass Dutch style houses and a pub then you come immediately to the Ferry. This should operate on demand (see Note 1 above). When you reach the west bank of the river, turn right and head northwest. You can walk either side of the canal. It runs parallel with the river and passes through nature reserves where the marshes are well managed.

In 1 kilometre go under the M5, happy to avoid the traffic and continue for nearly 2 kilometres to the A379. Cross with care to the canal towing path (the right hand path). In one kilometre you reach the Double Locks Pub where there are refreshments and toilets. You join the cycle way now to Salmonpool Bridge where you can cross to the east bank of the river..

Go across parkland, veering to the left where you have a good view of the weir then cross a final bridge to roadside. University buildings are on your right. Turn left and look for a twitten in the corner, avoiding Salmonpool La.

You now have a clear run through riverside parkland to the famous Exeter Quay where old warehouses have been converted into individual shops and cafes. Go to the end of the Quay and turn right. Climb the steps (for the car park) and a Walls Walk enables you to cross the busy Western Way. You then cross South Street to the lane opposite. Follow signs to the Cathedral.

From Exeter Cathedral either retrace your steps to Topsham or vary the route by staying on the east side of the Exe. If you decide on this course, take care as you approach M5 at High Tide the footpath may be flooded.

To return by bus, go to the High Street and head north to Paris Street. Turn right here and the bus station is down on the left. The 57 bus runs every 15 minutes, 30 minutes on a Sunday. (See note 4 above).

Walk 24: Castle Lane to Littleham and Exmouth (Coast Path)

A peaceful stroll along the old rail track leads to Exmouth`s first Church, then a lane to the seaside town, finally a climb to cliff tops and woodland

Starting Point: Castle Lane. Parking is allowed near the bend. From here head towards Salterton Rd. There is also an informal Car Park on the left.
GR044821 Map: OS Explorer 115 **Terrain:** Easy slopes down to Exmouth (some on roads), steeper slopes to the Coast Path. **Distance:** 10 Miles
Local Information: A circular bus route enables passengers to travel hourly every day from Sandy Bay to Littleham and Exmouth.
For more details of Stagecoach 95, Phone traveline 0871 200 22 33

The Churches
Parish Church of Littleham-cum-Exmouth, S Margaret and S. Andrew dates back to 1234 when the Bishop of Exeter granted the church to the Canons of Exeter. The chancel has survived from this period. There is a trefoil piscina in the north wall. The rest of the church is 15th century and has a castellated tower. There are four bays

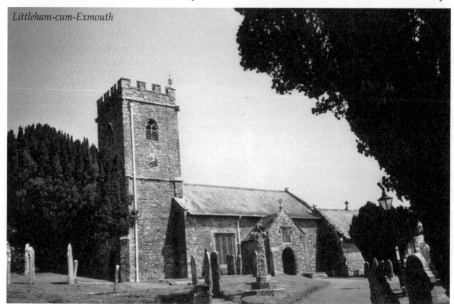

Littleham-cum-Exmouth

from the nave into the north or Drake Aisle of 1526. The glass in the central window depicts three figures: Jesus Christ with his crown of thorns, St Roch, patron saint of those suffering from the plague and the Archangel St Michael. The restored wagon roof has the original bosses including two Green Men. The rood screen, restored in

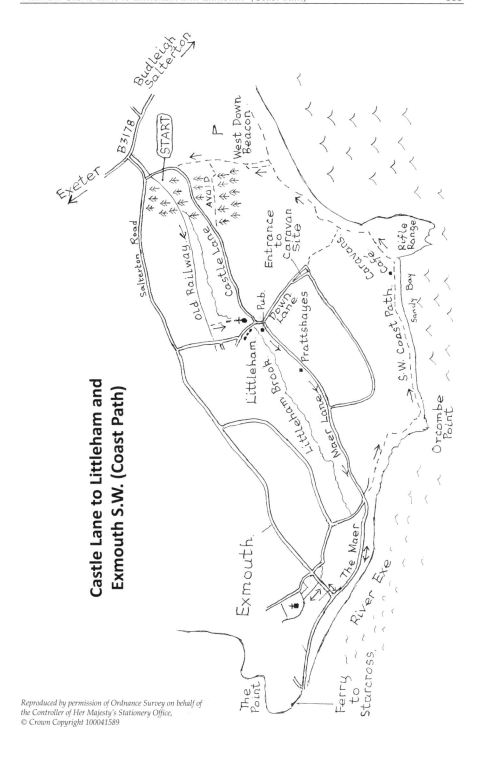

Castle Lane to Littleham and Exmouth S.W. (Coast Path)

1884, may have been brought from elsewhere. The south windows of the nave were enlarged in 1911. Outside the porch, a scratch dial has a sundial of 1780 above it. Stepping stones lead to the grave of Lady Nelson and her son. Her memorial by Turnerelli is in the chantry chapel. Standing high above Littleham Road, the church presents a perfect picture of a village church - now on the edge of suburbia.

Exmouth, Holy Trinity is an impressive building by G.H.F. Prynne of 1907, replacing a Victorian chapel. The builders of the first Holy Trinity on Chapel Hill in 1412 would be amazed to see this grand new church. It has tall arcades and much carving. The east window is high above a large carved reredos depicting the Assumption. The north chapel has an apsidal end. The Somerset type tower dominates this seaside town. The 21st century has its own spectacular modern equipment. A lift carries people up three stories to the care centre and library.

The Walk

At the top end of Castle Lane go through the small car park to a track leading to the disused railway between Exmouth and Budleigh Salterton. When you join this main track. Head southwest for 1 mile on this wide, firm, flat cycle route. At first you have the shelter of trees on either side and occasional picnic tables. The trees give way and views open on either side.

You see Littleham Church across fields on the left before you find the footpath there. Shortly after passing a footpath on the right, you turn left and cross two fields to the church. **From Littleham Church you have a choice:**

Walk to Exmouth. Go through the lychgate and turn left. In 75 metres cross to the local pub. Turn right into Maer Lane. This leads down to the sea front at Exmouth. Turn right and walk along the Esplanade as far as Carlton Hill. Turn right then second left into Louisa Place. Holy Trinity is the tallest church ahead.

Bus to Exmouth (Details above) Outside the church you can catch a bus in either direction. Buses go to Sandy Bay and the café on the sea front then return past the church to Exmouth. Hail whatever bus comes first.

From Holy Trinity go down to the Esplanade and turn left. Walk beside the sea on the right for about 1 mile. Soon after Maer Lane on the left, look out for the South West Coast Path sign. Turn left into this path which starts in an alley past suburban houses. You have a good climb up to the High Land of Orcombe overlooking the sea.

Pass stepping stones set into the ground to give examples of material from different geological ages. Here we are on red sandstone, typical of South Devon, witness the cliffs below. The path heads eastwards. Buttercups and green winged orchids can be seen in late spring in meadows on the left.

Continue on the cliff path for 1 kilometre. You reach Devon Cliffs Holiday Park and pass the caravans. At the lowest part of the cliff there is an attractive café overlooking the sea. You then have to veer left following the South West Coast Path and climb behind the Rifle Range at Straight Point.

After the last caravan you reach open cliffs again. Look out for sea birds, fulmars and gannets. After crossing a narrow leafy valley you are heading for West Down

Beacon. No need to climb to this point, unless you so wish. A path on the left along the base leads to the Golf Course. Avoid the signed path to Budleigh Salterton.

Head north through golfers and enter woodland. Take the path ahead signposted to Knowle. (**Not** the one to Littleham Church). In just under one kilometre you come out on the familiar corner of Castle Lane. The car park is ahead on the left.

Sandy Bay

Sandy Bay

Walk 25: Starcross to Powderham Castle, Powderham Church and Kenton

Many tracks lead to a magnificent medieval castle, glimpses of parkland, a parish church housing a treasure, an estate church and the Exe Estuary.

Starting Point: Starcross Rail Station next to Exmouth Ferry   **GR977819**
Map: OS Explorer 110 **Terrain:** Mainly flat, 1 hill   **Distance:** 6 Miles
Local Information: 1. Bus 2 runs from Exeter to Starcross every 15 minutes
Sundays every 30 mins. Less frequent in winter   Phone 01392 427711
2. Starcross – Exmouth ferry runs hourly, Apr. to Oct. Phone 07974 022536
3. For train times to Starcross, National Rail Enquiries: 08457 48 49 50
        Text phone: 0845 6050 600
Powderham Castle is medieval, the Courtenay family home since 1390. The castle continued to provide defense until 1645.
Open to the public Apr. to Nov. for a big entrance fee. Phone 01626 890243

The Churches

Kenton, All Saints is a 14th century Church in red sandstone with battlements on the tower, the two-storey porch, north and south aisles. The porch has niches and carved

Kenton

Kenton

Starcross to Kenton and Powderham

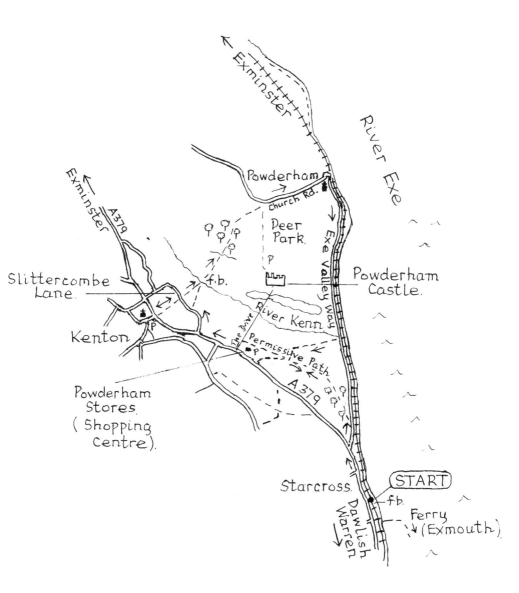

doorways. Inside, the church is spacious with 7 bays in Beer stone. The piers support capitals with a variety of carvings. The Lady Chapel is north of the chancel. The east window has six lights and the aisle windows have four lights. The 15th century pulpit was re-assembled in 1882 after it had been thrown out earlier that century. The great treasure of this church is the carved wooden rood screen, stretching across the east end, one of the finest in Devon. The lower panels have paintings of saints and apostles. It dates from 1455 and was beautifully restored 1899 – 1925 in memory of a member of the Courtenay family.

Powderham, St Clement stands on the edge of the castle estate, beside the River Exe. The north aisle is probably the extent of the original church of 1259. Today there is a nave, two aisles and chancel, all 15th century. The chancel screen has twelve Victorian panels depicting saints. The Perpendicular arcade in Beer stone can be dated to 1485. Margaret Courtenay claims to have paid for it. Fragments of 15th century glass are in the north aisle window. During the Civil War, Cromwell`s men made holes in the door for their muskets. That repaired door is now closed to visitors. You may be able to gain entry after a Sunday service, 11a.m. - 12 at present.

Powderham

The Walk

From the riverside, Starcross Station cross the footbridge to the road and turn right. Pass the pub on the left and toilets on the right. Keep beside the railway by the River Exe for ½ mile. Pass a green with picnic benches.

You are on Exe Valley Way, a cycle route shared here by cars. You can soon leave the tarmac. Turn left at a light grey villa where a sign for cyclists and walkers points to the permissive path to 'Powderham Store' (a shop at the entrance to Powderham Castle). On this permissive path saunter through woodland to emerge at flat fields and a view of the castle.

You cross the public footpath and continue on the wide track to the store and car park. Pass these on your left and you come immediately to the entrance to Powderham Castle (see Note 4 above). *Turn right for the castle.*

Turn left for the village of Kenton. A short length of the drive brings you to the main road. Turn right and walk beside the road (about 150 metres) with a cement coated wall for company on your right.

Turn right at the first lane and pass a road into a housing estate on the left. Avoid this and follow the lane, Slittercombe Lane. It turns left and provides a quiet route around the northeast edge of Kenton. Avoid the first path on the right. At the next **junction** in 250 metres, turn left. A narrow twitten leads beside a ditch to the Church. First, you have to cross the A379 to a side road to the Church.

From Kenton Church return to the twitten and retrace your steps to the **junction**. Keep straight on over managed swampy ground. Cross the footbridge over the River Kenn and continue to a track at the base of a wooded hill. A private entrance to Powderham Estate is on the right.

Our footpath, excluded from the Estate by high rails, is clearly defined. It leads uphill through the edge of woodland. You climb out of the wood, over a ridge and down to Church Road and another private entrance to the castle.

Turn right and walk along the straight Ilex Avenue to the facing church. The church is closed except for services.

Go behind Powderham Church to climb to the straight cycle route and turn right. You are on the Exe Valley Way again at a more northerly point, heading south. The railway is on the left and the swampy estate land on the right. You can keep straight on for the ferry at Starcross.

Or in nearly 1 kilometre turn right at public footpath sign. Cross water meadows heading west towards Powderham Castle again. At the familiar junction, turn left into the permissive path and return through woodland to the grey villa. Turn right and retrace your steps to the station and ferry.

Walk 26: Exminster to Kenn

Country lanes and footpaths link two ancient churches near Exeter.

Starting Point: Bus Stop and Victory Hall Car Park Exminster **GR**946876
Map: OS Explorer 110   **Terrain:** country lanes and footpaths, some hills
Distance: 5½ Miles
Local Information:
  1. **Bus 2** every 20 mins Exeter to Newton Abbot calls in at Exminster
  2. Towsington Barton is an old farmhouse, updated in 17th century.
  3. Old Dawlish Road is the ancient route from Exeter to Dawlish.
  4. Ley Arms, Kenn is basically 17th century, much extended.

The Churches

Note: The Courtenays were Earls of Devon in 1335 and had influence on these churches for 2½ centuries. Born locally, William Courtenay became Archbishop of Canterbury 1381- 1396. See Note 4 on Powderham Castle

   St Martin`s Church, Exminster is built in pinkish Breccia stone. Nothing remains of the Saxon Minster, founded in 8th century. In its place here is a heavily restored

Exminster

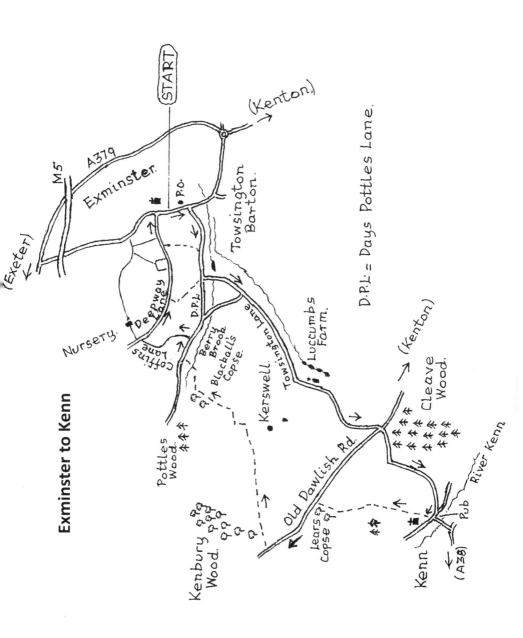

Perpendicular church. The tower in Breccia ashlar has three stories and a stair turret. The grand ring of eight bells of Exminster are famous. The nave has Perpendicular windows in the north and a 19th century ceiled wagon roof. The 15th century south aisle has arches resting on sandstone pillars, three of which are monoliths. The chancel has a three-light early 19th century window. There is a late medieval 10 bay rood screen. Also the parclose screen between chancel and Lady Chapel is 15th century. Most impressive is the plaster ceiling of the Peamore or Lady Chapel of 1633. It depicts the 12 Apostles, the 4 Evangelists, the Nativity, the Cross and Resurrection. A wall monument to Otho Petre of Bohay (died 1607) and his family is in the chancel.

Kenn

The Parish Church of St Andrew, Kenn is first mentioned in a charter in 12th century. It was already dedicated to St Andrew. The Norman font may be from this early church. The basin is formed from a square of Purbeck marble, hollowed and rounded inside. It has a central column with black polished corner columns. The chancel with 5–light Decorated east window was built in 13th century. The tower was also added then. The original west doorway to the tower stands northeast in the cemetery. It has the fashionable ball flower carving of the period. A chantry of 1280 had a priest to sing masses for Hugh de Courtenay. It is now St John`s Chapel. When chantries were abolished in 16th century, the priest was probably evicted from Chappel Court. We pass this thatched house when we leave the church on our walk. St Andrew`s was again enlarged in 15th century and has retained the exterior in local red Heavitree stone. It has battlements throughout. Walls were pierced in order to add north and south aisles. The octagonal piers are formed of monolyths. The windows are Perpendicular. The wagon roof of the chancel is of that period. The screen, dated 1500, has survived mainly intact. It has elaborate tracery and under each archway there are 4 panels. 44 saints are painted on these panels. The colourful stained glass was planned as a set depicting New Testament scenes. It was the project of Revd. R. Porter (1858) and realised by Hardman of Birmingham. Only the vestry window has medieval glass.

The Walk

From Victory Hall Car Park and Bus Stop turn right and head north for the nearby Church. Then return south on the pavement down the Main Road, passing the Post Office on the left.

Take the first turning right into Days Pottles Lane. *No pavemnt here so take care.* In just over ¼ mile turn left into the delightful Towsington Lane. It passes Towsington Barton on the left, crosses Berry Brook and takes a southwest course through rolling countryside and gentle slopes. In 1 kilometre it passes farm buildings, Kerswell, *or Cresswell,* on the right and Luccumbs on the left. Continue to crossroads.

Cross Old Dawlish Road to the steeply sloping narrow lane opposite. You sink through Cleave Wood and, after two bends, come down to the riverside village of Kenn. The white pub near the River Kenn is popular Ley Arms.

Turn right for Kenn Church and climb steps to go through the lychgate to the South Porch.

To return to Exminster, from the southeast corner, near the road, a path passes through the churchyard. It heads northwards up through fields and past woodland back to Old Dawlish Road that follows the top of a ridge.

This path used to lead to Kerswell Farm. That section is now alas closed.

Turn left and walk along the ridge of Old Dawlish Road. In ¼ mile turn right into a footpath just before Kenbury Wood, partly used as a landfill site.

Head eastwards on an elevated path above Kerswell to the right. In 1 kilometre turn sharp left then right through ancient fields where crop marks show prehistoric activity. Pass Pottles Wood on the left then veer right and left to re-cross Berry Brook.

At Days Pottles Lane, turn right and walk for under ¼ mile to Coffins Lane on the left. This narrow winding lane takes you up to Deepway Lane.

Turn right and follow Deepway Lane for 1 mile back to Exminster.

Walk 27: Crediton to Shobrooke

From the first Cathedral in Devon walk over fields and then through a private estate with lakes and rare trees to a modest church and pretty hamlet

Starting Point: Car Park for the swimming pool and leisure centre, Crediton GR843004 **Map:** OSExplorer 114   **Terrain:** Mainly flat   **Distance:** 5-6 Miles
Note: This is a linear walk. You walk there and back on the same route.
Local Information: Crediton is a small town above the River Yeo. The little rail station is near the river. The town has an air of the 1950s.
Shobrooke Park has seen a succession of homes. The first was built for Sir William Periam (1535-1605). In 1820 a house by Hakewill replaced it. This became a school that burnt down in 1947. There is now a modest modern house but access to the parkland is limited to public rights of way. Phone Jack Shelley if you wish to see a Folly and extend your walk. 07971 136901

The Churches

Church of the Holy Cross, Crediton. Winfrith, who studied as a monk at Exeter, was born in Crediton around 680 A.D. He made an impact as a missionary here and in Europe. The Pope canonised him as St Boniface. So it is not surprising that a Minster was established here in 739 A.D. King Aethelheard gave 'Cridie' to the Bishop of Sherborne. In 909 the diocese of Sherborne was divided and Crediton became a Cathedral. The first Bishop here was Eadulf. Aethelstan confirmed the Diocese of Crediton in 933. Nine bishops succeeded here until Leofric moved the See to Exeter in 1050. Then Crediton became a collegiate church with 18 canons and 18 vicars. Their chapter house can be seen off the southeast part of the church. In 1547 when King Edward dissolved collegiates, the parishioners bought the church for £200. The church then had governors, 9 from Crediton and 3 from Sandford. They held meetings in the second floor of the chapter house. Remains of the 12th century church can be seen in the shape of the present building. The east part is as big as the nave. The lower

Crediton

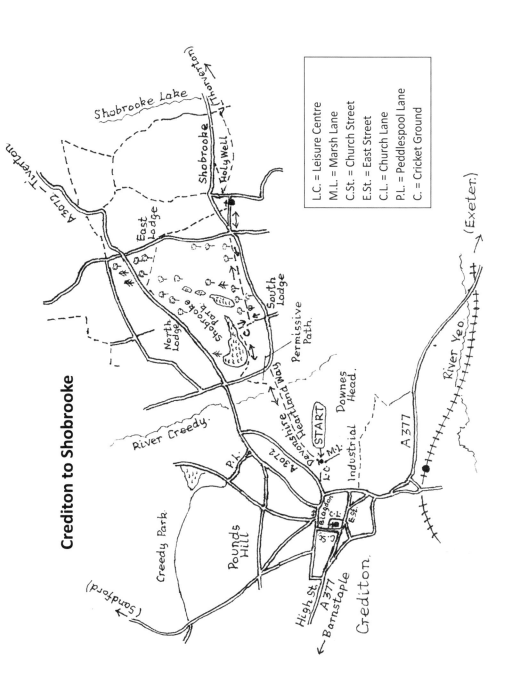

L.C. = Leisure Centre
M.L. = Marsh Lane
C.St. = Church Street
E.St. = East Street
C.L. = Church Lane
P.L. = Peddlespool Lane
C. = Cricket Ground

Crediton to Shobrooke

Shobrooke

part of the tower and the piers at the crossing are 12th century. The font is Norman. The church, neglected in 1413, had revived by 1471. It is built using the rich red stone of the Posbury quarries. The east end, once the college chapel, was the first to be rebuilt in the early 15th century. It has five bays. The altar is in front of a wall, dividing it from the Lady Chapel of 1250. From 1572 to 1860 this separate space behind the altar was used as a grammar school. The Perpendicular nave with six bays was built of local stone from Thorverton. The clerestory was added also in 15th century. The fine Perpendicular west window has been imitated. In 1874 the Victorians replaced the east window, already Perpendicular, with another to match the west window. There is much else of interest and I suggest you buy the official guide booklet.

Shobrooke, St Swithun stands on high ground away from the village. There is a nearby Holy Well. The church was built of local red raddon stone in Perpendicular style. The north aisle is 14th century and the handsome tower 15th century. The Victorians added a south aisle to match the north. The 12th century south doorway may have been relocated, then a porch added. The doorway in Thorverton stone has shafts with scalloped capitals. The Victorian stained glass is good.

The Walk

From the Leisure Centre you have to walk into town to see the Parish Church. Go to the main road, A3072 and turn left. Cross diagonally left to another busy road heading uphill – at least there is a pavement. Turn left as soon as you can and head for the large red imposing church. Return to base.

From the Leisure Centre find a path in the left corner heading east through sports` fields, flanking new houses on the left. You are on the Devonshire Heartland Way. Leave the houses, keeping on course over two flat fields. The footpath crosses a ditch and then another small field where a thin footbridge takes you over Mill Leat. In the last field, instead of following the footpath straight ahead leading to the road, turn left onto a permissive path that crosses the field diagonally and brings you to a stile opposite Shobrooke Park. This avoids a road walk.

Inside Shobrooke Park, veer to the right up a gentle slope towards a lake where fishermen vie with egrets and geese for the fish. Follow the lake on your left as far as a grand private bridge at the head. You cannot cross the bridge. Stay on your side of the lake and go through a kissing gate into light woodland.

Turn right to pass a cricket pitch. Head towards gates at South Lodge. Just short of the gates, turn left and enter an avenue. Here is a gravel path climbing gently uphill under the trees. In nearly ½ mile you reach another gate and leave Shobrooke Park here. The exit is on the right.

You come out to crossroads. The Church is signed straight ahead. For the village of Shobrooke and the pub, go past the church and turn left then right.

To return to Crediton, the pleasantest route is back through the park. You may vary the route a little by keeping to the left of the avenue but you have to turn right at South Lodge and go back to the lake. Retrace your steps to the entrance and back over fields to Crediton.

Walk 28: Sidbury to Harpford

A hilly walk through history, following the East Devon way.

Starting Point: Car Park at Ridgeway, NW Sidbury **GR**138918
Map: OS Explorer 115 **Terrain:** Hilly, some woodland, mainly traffic free
Distance: 10 Miles
Local Information: Sidbury Castle is a large Iron Age Hill Fort overlooking the town and the River Sid.
Note: Unofficial paths on Core Hill may cause confusion. Bring a compass!

The Churches

Sidbury, St Giles

Tours of the Church are arranged on Thursdays at 2.30 p.m. in summer, followed by a tour of the 7th century crypt at 3.30 p.m. Phone 01395 597324

The Church Guide is very thorough and may fill in some gaps below.

Sidbury is famous for its Saxon Crypt of around 670 A.D. It contained an even earlier fragment, probably part of a preaching cross once erected by Irish monks who first converted the Saxon heathens in 6th century. The Normans, determined to show their superior skills at church building, rebuilt many Saxon churches. In Sidbury some of the rubble from the demolished walls was thrown into the crypt. By 1073 Sidbury was under the Norman Priory of St Nicholas, Exeter. The generous size of the nave has not changed since then, suggesting a flourishing community here. First the chancel was replaced, then the bell tower built in 1150. The string courses on the outer walls of the tower are typical of the Romanesque period. There are battlements around the needle spire. Two Norman figures were later built into the tower. They are believed to represent St Giles and St Peter. Inside the tower the

Sidbury

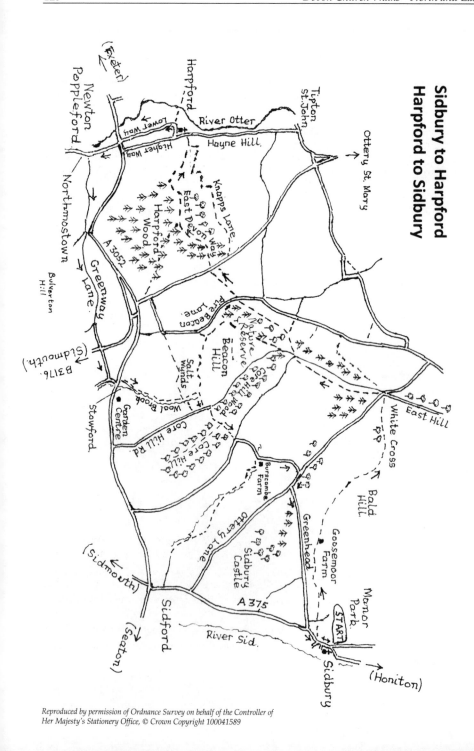

vestibule has a vault roof and four Norman corbels. Vaulted ceilings are in the nave, transepts and aisles and a variety of carved corbels. The walls of the nave were pierced and made into arcades for the north and south aisles in 1190. The chancel arch was also changed then to Transitional style. Some windows in the chancel are Decorated. The Perpendicular window in the south wall of the chancel has modern glass of St Giles and St Peter. The transepts escaped destruction and had Early English windows inserted around 1250. In 15th century a grand two-storey porch, crenellated parapets and two turreted stairways were added. There are two grotesque animal gargoyles on the porch buttresses. The font is also Perpendicular.

Harpford, St Gregory was held in 1205 by the Abbey of St Michael Monte and then later by Sion Monastery. The Church was rebuilt 1883 – 4, keeping to the original 13th century building of red rubble with lancet windows. The north aisle dates from 14th century with octagonal piers and square headed windows. The tower is 15th century. The south aisle is Victorian as is much of the stained glass. Fortunately it is of good quality, some by Kempe, with attractive colours. The churchyard cross of 1778 remembers Augustus Toplady who wrote the hymn, 'Rock of Ages'.

The Walk

From the Car Park head south down the main road, passing the shop on the right and the Church on the left. At a telephone booth turn right into a track that carries the East Devon Way. Head westwards into the hills.

At crosstracks keep straight on. *The private driveway on the right with a handsome avenue of Lime trees, leads to the Manor House.* Our stony track is well defined. When you come to damp grassy slopes down to a stream, you take the gate on the left into a farm track and turn right to pass the stream on your right. Then rejoin the track up to pass Goosemoor Farm on the right and start climbing. The track is enclosed and in ½ mile it is a relief to come out into a high field beside Bald Hill where trees belie its name!

Continue up the middle of the field until you come to a post with a marker. It points to an elevated path overlooking the valley on the left. Enjoy the views of pastureland sprinkled with trees. Pass a copse on the left and cross a flat field to a gate in the trees. At the top road White Cross is to the right.

You turn left to pick up the East Devon Way (EDW) as it heads south through a wood. When you come out of the wood, keep on course across an open field with trees on your right.

As you enter Fire Beacon Nature Reserve, ignore the bridleway on the left and keep to East Devon Way. In over a mile from White Cross you meet Fire Beacon Lane.

Turn right then left, going down some steps into a field. Head for the right hand corner and keep straight on to a gate into a **metalled road.** Cross to another gate into Harpford Wood.

Follow the clear path through the wood. You are still on East Devon Way. *Parts are slippery if wet.* It leads under a disused railway bridge and continues through the wood to a **metalled road,** 1 mile from that above.

Turn left passing Littlecot House. Turn left into the next lane where a gate in the wall leads to the Church of St Gregory the Great, Harpford.

Leave the churchyard by the south gate. Turn right to follow Lower Lane as it heads south towards A3052.

Cross to the lane opposite, passing Bridge End Cottage. Immediately before Northmostown Farm, take the unmarked lane on the left. In under ½ mile, the lane again draws close to the A3052. Avoid turning to the right up to Bulverton Hill. Take the stony lane with the sign 'Unsuitable for motor Vehicles'. Continue for ½ mile to B3176. Cross this road and keep to Greenway Lane.

At the end of the lane turn left onto a narrow verge. Turn left again and cross the A3052 to metalled lane marked 'Public Footpath' and you have a climb ahead. Ignore stiles on the left then the right. In 1 mile of gentle climb from the road you come to a crossing path.

Turn right to cross a footbridge and stile into a field. Head west across the field to Core Hill Road. Turn left then fork right on a footpath into trees. *Here you may need a compass. Your direction is mainly northeast.*

Climb gradually up to a ridge. Take a footpath downhill, go through a gate and across a field for a stile into a lane at a bend. Continue northeast along the lane, passing Burscombe Farm on the right.

In ½ mile you reach a T-junction of lanes. Turn right and then left for the lane back to Sidbury, approximately 1 mile away. At A375 turn left for the car park. You pass the Church of St Giles on the way.

Bibliography

***Devon* -** by W.G. Hoskins
    David and Charles, Newton Abbot and London - First published in 1954

***Devon`s Churches* -** Canon Professor Nicholas Orme
    Cloister Books

***Some Old Devon Churches* -** J. Stabb
    1908 – 16 London

***Walks in Historic Devon* -** Michael Bennie
    2001 Countryside Books, Berks

***Slow Devon and Exmoor* -** Hilary Bradt
    Bradt Travel Guides

***The Buildings of England - Devon* -** Bridget Cherry and Nikolaus Pevsner
    (1952 Penguin) 2004 Yale University Press for The Buildings Books Trust

***Betjeman's Best British Churches* -** Updated by Richard Surman
    (1958) 2011 Harper Collins

***Harris`s Guide to Churches and Cathedrals* -** Brian L. Harris
    Random House Publishing

***England's Thousand Best Churches* -** Simon Jenkins
    1999 Allen Lane, Penguin Press

See `Devon Church Walks - South and West` for long distance footpaths

Notes